Saline District Library

Provided by
a grant
from the

**CARL F. SCHRANDT
ENDOWMENT
FUND**

PUPPETS AND PUPPET THEATRE

David Currell

The Crowood Press

First published in 1999 by
The Crowood Press Ltd
Ramsbury, Marlborough
Wiltshire SN8 2HR

British Library Cataloguing in Publication Data

A catalogue record for this book is available from the British Library.

ISBN 1 86126 135 7

To Emily Ayşa and Alexander Emre, my children, who love puppet theatre.

Photo Credits
Courtesy John M. Blundall, Puppet Theatre Consultant, The Scottish Mask and Puppet Theatre Centre, Glasgow: 35, 136
(a) (b) (c) (d) (e) (f), 169 (a) (b) (c); courtesy Coomber Electronic Equipment Ltd, Worcester: 196 (a) (b) (c); courtesy Ray &
Joan DaSilva, DaSilva Puppet Company, Bicester, Oxfordshire: 165 (b), 202, 206; courtesy Mary Edwards, The Puppet
Factory Ltd., Far Forest, Worcestershire: 4, 42, 43; Steve Finch, courtesy Puppet Centre Trust, London (Hogarth
Collection) and Salford Museum & Art Gallery: 38; Steve Finch, courtesy Puppet Centre Trust, London (on loan to
touring exhibition, courtesy Jim Henson Productions) and Salford Museum & Art Gallery: 6; Chris Lawrenson, courtesy
Lyndie Wright, Little Angel Theatre, London:182, 203; Philippe Mangen, courtesy Puppet Centre Trust, London (on loan
to touring exhibition, courtesy John Blundall, Scottish Mask & Puppet Theatre Centre): 10, 39; courtesy Puppet Centre
Trust, London (Crafts Council Collection): 36; courtesy Puppet Centre Trust, London (Jessica Souhami Archive): 128 (b);
courtesy Ian Purves, International Purves Puppets, Biggar, Lanarkshire, Scotland: 195 (a) (b); John Roberts, courtesy
Lyndie Wright, Little Angel Theatre, London: 99; David Rose, author's collection: 5, 9, 32, 37, 52, 59, 79, 110 (b) (c) (d),
138 (a) (b), 140 (e), 153 (c) (d) (e), 190 (a), 117, 118, 119, 120, 130, 133, 186, 188, 189; David Rose, courtesy Puppet Centre
Trust, London: 16, 19 (a) (b), 69; David Rose, courtesy Puppet Centre Trust, London (Barry Smith Collection): 7, 21, 22,
26, 33, 53, 58; David Rose, courtesy Puppet Centre Trust, London (Crafts Council Collection): 15; David Rose, courtesy
Puppet Centre Trust, London (Hogarth Collection): 1, 2, 3, 17, 103; courtesy Albrecht Roser, Stuttgart, Germany: 198;
Stephen Sharples, courtesy Christopher Leith, London: 128 (a); Stephen Sharples, courtesy Lyndie Wright, Little Angel
Theatre, London: 6,44; Barry Smith, author's photograph collection: 27, 165 (a), 201; Barry Smith, courtesy Puppet
Centre Trust, London (Barry Smith Collection): 11, 13, 68, 171, 172; David Stanfield, courtesy Lyndie Wright, Little
Angel Theatre, London: 8, 46, 61, 62, 65, 102, 200; courtesy Strand Lighting Ltd., Middlesex: 187 (a) (b) (c) (d), 192, 194
(a) (b); courtesy Lyndie Wright, Little Angel Theatre, London: 47, 123, 124, 191, 199, 205; courtesy Zero 88 Lighting Ltd.,
Cwmbran, Gwent: 193; courtesy Puppet Centre Trust, London: 24.

Typeset by Annette Findlay
Printed and bound by Leo Paper Products, China

Contents

Acknowledgements

Puppeteers world-wide are generous in sharing their knowledge, skills and experience, and I have been extremely fortunate to benefit from this generosity in the preparation of Puppets and Puppet Theatre.

For information on their approaches to puppet making and performing, as well as for photographs, I am indebted to John Blundall, Ray DaSilva, Mary Edwards, Geoff Felix, Christopher Leith, Ian Purves and Lyndie Wright. Technical information on lighting and sound has been received from Sue Davies and Bill Richards of Strand Lighting Limited, Claire House of Zero 88 Lighting Limited, and Mark Piatkowski of Coomber Electronic Equipment Limited. Others who have contributed photographs are listed separately.

My very sincere thanks are due to David Rose, a friend, colleague, and photographer, who has been extremely generous with his time and expertise, and has made it possible to include so many colourful and informative photographs.

I am grateful also to Loretta Howells (Director), Allyson Kirk and Glen Alexander of the Puppet Centre Trust, London, who have provided reference resources, technical information and photographs, and made available the Trust's extensive collections for photography.

The late Barry Smith, Director of the Theatre of Puppets and Ray DaSilva, Co-Director of the DaSilva Puppet Company, shared their individual approaches to puppet performance for a previous book, which is embedded also in the present work. I therefore acknowledge with gratitude the major contributions made to the performance chapter by each of these puppet masters.

Finally, I am extremely grateful to the team at The Crowood Press, who have been enthusiastic and supportive, and helped to make the book a pleasure to write.

1 An Introduction to Puppet Theatre

PUPPET THEATRE HERITAGE

Puppetry and puppet theatre have a long and fascinating heritage. The origins of this visual and dramatic art are thought to lie mainly in the East, although exactly when or where it originated is not known. It may have been practised in India 4000 years ago: impersonation was forbidden by religious taboo and the leading player in Sanskrit plays is termed *sutradhara* ('the holder of strings'), so it is likely that puppets existed before human actors.

In China, marionettes were in use by the eighth century AD and shadow puppets date back well over 1000 years. The Burmese puppet theatre had a significant influence on the development of the human dance drama, and a dancer's skill is still judged on his or her ability to re-create the movements of a marionette. And Chikamatsu Monzaemon (1653-1725), Japan's finest dramatist, wrote not for human theatre, but for the *Bunraku* puppets (*see* Fig 24), which

Fig 1 Javanese *wayang golek* rod puppets

Fig 2 An Indian marionette from the Rajasthan region

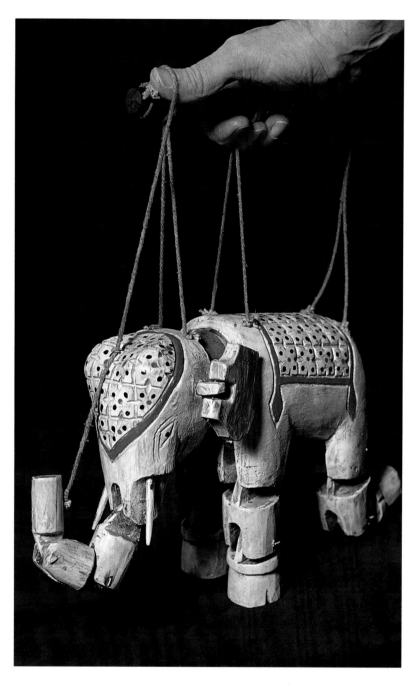

Fig 3 A traditional carved Burmese marionette

as 800 BC, and puppet theatre was a common entertainment – probably with marionettes and glove puppets – in Greece and Rome by 400 BC, according to the writings of the time. In the Middle Ages, puppets were widely used to enact the scriptures until they were banned by the Council of Trent. Since the Renaissance, puppetry in Europe has continued as an unbroken tradition.

Sicilian puppets – knights one metre (three feet) high, wearing beaten armour and operated from above with rods (*see* Fig 32) – have performed the story of *Orlando Furioso* since the sixteenth century, but this type of puppet was, in fact, in use as long ago as Roman times. In Germany, puppets have performed *The History of Doctor Faustus* since 1587, and in France marionette operas became so popular that in 1720 the live opera attempted to have them restricted by law. The eighteenth-century French *Ombres Chinoises* shadow puppets were not only a fairground entertainment but were popular among artists and in the fashionable world.

In England, puppets were certainly known by the fourteenth century and, during the Civil War, when theatres were closed, puppet theatre enjoyed a period of unsurpassed popularity. By the early eighteenth century it was a fashionable entertainment for the wealthy, and in the late nineteenth century England's marionette troupes, considered to be the best in the world, toured the globe with their elaborate productions.

The ubiquitous Mr Punch originated in Italy. A puppet version of Pulcinella, a buffoon in the Italian *Commedia dell' Arte*, was carried throughout Europe by the wandering showmen and a similar character – including Petruschka (Russia), Pickle Herring, later Jan Klaasen (Holland), and Polichinelle (France) – became established in many

once overshadowed the *Kabuki* in popularity.

In Europe, the puppet drama flourished in the early Mediterranean civilizations and under Roman rule. The Greeks may have used puppets as early

countries. The French version was introduced to England in 1660 with the return of Charles II; it became Punchinello, soon shortened to Punch, and enjoyed such popularity that he began to be included in all manner of plays. By 1825, Punch was at the height of his popularity, and the story in which he played had taken on its standard basic form.

In the nineteenth century the puppet show was taken to America by emigrants from many European countries, and their various national traditions laid the foundations for the great variety of styles found there today.

Eastern Europe had early traditions of travelling puppet-showmen but, with a few exceptions, puppetry did not develop significantly there until the twentieth century. However, it then progressed at an impressive rate.

The twentieth century has brought new materials and techniques to puppet theatre, and has seen a revival of interest in the art through television and film, as well as a renewed emphasis on the quality of live performances. Official recognition of puppetry as a performance art has now been achieved.

THE NATURE OF THE PUPPET

The survival of puppet theatre over some 4000 years owes a great deal to man's fascination with the inanimate object animated in a dramatic manner, and to the very special way in which puppet theatre involves its audience. Through the merest hint or suggestion in a movement – perhaps just a tilt of the head – the spectator is invited to invest the puppet with emotion and movement, and to see it 'breathe'.

A puppet is not an actor, and puppet theatre is not human theatre in miniature. In many ways, puppet theatre has more in common with dance and mime than with acting. Puppet theatre depends more upon action and less upon the spoken word than the actor does; generally, it cannot handle complex soul-searching, and it is denied many of the aspects of non-verbal communication that are available to the actor. But the puppet, still or moving, can be just as powerful as the actor.

The actor *represents* but the puppet *is*. The puppet brings to the performance just what you want and no more; it has no identity outside its performance, and brings no other associations on to the stage. The puppet is free from many human physical limitations and can speak the unspeakable, and deal with taboos. The power and potential of the puppet has attracted

Fig 4 Pulcinella, a large marionette, as he first appeared in England, re-created for television by Mary Edwards. The head is carved in jelutong wood

artists such as Molière, Cocteau, Klee, Shaw, Mozart, Gordon Craig, Goethe and Lorca who have all taken a serious interest in this art – one of the most liberating forms of theatre.

TYPES OF PUPPET AND STAGING

Most types of puppet in use today fall into four broad categories – hand or glove puppets, rod puppets, marionettes and shadow puppets – but there is a variety of combinations. Among these are glove-rod, hand-rod, rod-hand and rod-marionette puppets, detailed in Chapter 2. There is also a wide range of other related techniques, from masks to finger puppets, from the toy theatre to animated puppet film.

The glove puppet is used like a glove on the operator's hand; the term 'hand puppet' is sometimes used synonymously but here it describes figures where the whole hand is inserted into the puppet's head. Glove puppets are quite simple in structure but hand puppets often have a costumed human hand, or arms and hands operated by rods. These puppets, although limited in gesture to the movement of one's hand, are ideal for quick, robust action and can be most expressive. The live hand inside the puppet gives it a unique flexibility of physique.

The rod puppet is held and moved by rods, usually from below but sometimes from above; those in the Japanese *Bunraku* style require two or three operators, who hold the puppet in front of them. Rod puppets vary in complexity, ranging from a simple shape supported on a single stick to a fully articulated figure. They offer potential for creativity in design and presentation, and their range of swift and subtle movements enables them to deliver anything from sketches to large dramatic pieces.

The marionette is a puppet on strings, suspended from a control held by the puppeteer. It is versatile and can be simple or complex in both construction and control. Performances can be graceful and charming, and fast and forceful action is generally avoided. For manipulation, the experienced puppeteer draws upon the marionette's natural movements to great advantage.

Shadow puppets are normally flat cut-out figures held against a translucent, illuminated screen. The term is also used loosely to describe full-colour, translucent figures operated in the same manner. Shadow puppets are ideally suited to the illustration of a narrated story, but they can also handle direct dialogue and vigorous knockabout action.

Increasingly, puppeteers are exploring the use of space instead of restricting themselves to the confines of the conventional booth or stage. However, glove and rod puppets are usually presented from within a booth. The traditional covered booth is still used for 'Punch and Judy', but an open booth without a proscenium has become popular for other shows; it affords far greater scope for performance, and a wider viewing angle.

Marionette variety acts are frequently presented on an open stage with the puppeteer in view. The large marionette stage with a proscenium to hide the operators tends to be used for plays in more permanent situations: size, portability and setting-up time are factors that have influenced the trend towards open-stage performances. Although shadow puppets are generally limited to performing against a translucent screen, a great deal of inge-

Fig 5 A Chinese style of glove puppet

Fig 6 Oscar the Grouch, a hand puppet designed and made by Don Sahlin for *Sesame Street*. It is made of foam, covered in fleece and synthetic fur fabric

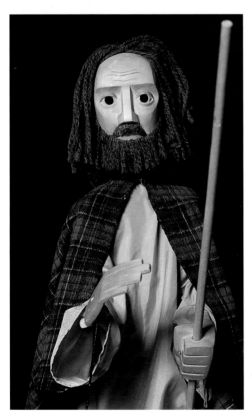

Fig 7 Joseph, from the Nativity, a carved wooden rod puppet of unknown origin

Fig 8 Aunt Rebecca, designed and carved by John Wright for *A Trumpet for Nap*, the Little Angel Theatre

Fig 9 Chinese shadow puppets created in leather, which is treated to make it translucent and coloured with dyes

nuity has been displayed by performers in their use of multiple screens, projections, superimposed images and the like.

It is possible to combine or alternate the use of different types of puppet in one performance. Used with other puppets, shadow play can illustrate linking narrative, portray distant action and, for example, dream, memory and underwater sequences. However, the staging demands of some puppet combinations can be considerable.

USING THIS BOOK

This book covers fundamental principles of puppet anatomy and design, extensive details of puppet construction and every aspect of the performance, including staging, lighting and sound.

Many aspects of the design and construction of the puppet are interdependent. For example, decisions about the performance will affect the type of puppet and staging methods to be used, and a head cannot be made for a rod puppet or marionette until it has been decided how the neck is to be joined to the body or whether the neck is to be created separate from, or integral to, the head. It is important, therefore, to design and make the puppet according to the advice given in all of the chapters; try to resist the temptation to launch into making a puppet with little idea of what the puppet will be required to do. Time spent reading and planning will be a worthwhile investment.

2 The Anatomy of a Puppet

PRINCIPLES OF DESIGN

The puppet is both an essence and an emphasis of the character it is intended to reflect. The puppet artist has to create and interpret character, not imitate it, so the puppeteer's art involves simplification and selection, and offers freedom not only to design the costumes of the actors, but also to create their heads, faces, body shapes, and so on.

You need to create a puppet that looks and moves like the character you wish to convey. Plan a project, however simply, and know what the puppet is to be and do, then you can design a specific puppet for that purpose. (Remember, it may be necessary to explore different techniques as the puppet progresses.)

Often beginners make puppets by drawing upon what they think they know about people: they make children small, adults bigger, and try to convey all the character in the face. The result is puppets that are less than convincing. You must conceive the design as a whole, and for this you need to *observe and analyse* what you see. Like an artist, study natural form and interpret it by searching for the underlying structures and working on these. Look to the basic structure, and see how it gets its form.

In principle, keep your designs bold and simple, with clean lines, to

Fig 10 The Devil as Herdsman from Stravinsky's *The Soldier's Tale*, the Little Angel Theatre. Designed and made by Lyndie Wright using polystyrene covered with pearl glue and brown paper; string is used to edge the sculpting. The hands were made on a wire armature using celastic, which is no longer suitable for puppets; leather would be used instead now

Fig 11 Anonymous, a hand puppet with a cast head designed and made by Barry Smith for his Theatre of Puppets' production, *A Variety of People*. Now in the Puppet Centre Barry Smith Collection

achieve greater dramatic effect; delicate features, however beautiful, will be lost on the puppet stage. A puppet that lacks bold design may appear nondescript from only a few feet away, while too much facial detail may hinder the conveying of character. Also note the importance of the eyes; they bring the face to life perhaps more than any other single feature.

It is useful to keep a scrapbook for inspiration and ideas: include drawings, pictures of people of all ages and types, in uniform or costume, features, cartoons, and articles, for example, on make-up or hair styles.

PROPORTION AND DESIGN

Strict adherence to the 'rules' of proportion does not make an interesting and effective puppet, while a puppet made to human proportions looks unnatural. However, it is worth considering certain guidelines with regard to proportion.

The adult human head is approximately one-seventh of a person's height; for a puppet, it is often about one-fifth, but could be any size you choose. On humans and puppets, the hand is approximately the same size as the distance from the chin to the middle of the forehead, and covers most of the face. The hand is also the same length as the forearm and as the upper arm; feet are a little longer. Elbows are level with the waist, the wrist with the bottom of the body and the fingertips half-way down the thigh. The body is generally a little shorter than the legs.

Pay attention also to the bulk of the body and the limbs. A common mistake is to make the puppet too tall and thin, lacking any real body shape, particularly in profile. Hold the puppet between a strong light and a blank wall and examine the shadows it casts: strongly designed puppets will create strong, interesting shadows. Ensure that the neck, arms and legs have sufficient bulk in relation to the head and body. Even when covered with clothes, it is noticeable if limbs are too skinny.

The head can be divided into four approximately equal parts – the chin to the nose; the nose to the eyes; the eyes to the hairline; and the hairline to the top of the skull, which is slightly less than the other sections. The eyes are approximately half-way between the chin and the top of the skull. The top and bottom of the ears are normally in line with the top and bottom of the nose.

Avoid putting the eyes too high in the head or too close together, the forehead too low, and the ears too high or too small for the head. Ears should be studied from the side and from behind: they contribute to characterization more than might be imagined. Viewed in profile, the neck is not in the centre of the head but set further back and possibly angled, depending on character.

However, it is the variations from the norm which are usually most significant in creating a dramatically effective character. For example, the spacing of the eyes depends upon the width of the nose and the characterization required. The age of a character affects the proportions of the head. 'Hair' can completely change the head's apparent shape, so consider the bulking of your chosen hair material when shaping the skull; different materials, such as thick synthetic fur or dyed string, will have

varying influences upon size, shape and, therefore, character.

The angle at which the head sits on the body and the way in which it moves are essential to characterization, so it is important to consider these points with regard to the positioning of joints between the head, neck and body.

PUPPET STRUCTURE

Glove Puppets

Glove puppets are constrained in size and design by the need to contain a human hand. The operator's wrist becomes the puppet's waist, so it is important to have a long 'glove' almost to the elbow, so that your arm does not show while performing. Use a dark material to help it recede, or a neutral colour, if that blends in more effectively.

The neck is usually slightly bell-bottomed, to assist in securing the glove body. The recommended method of operation is with index and middle fingers in the neck, thumb in one arm, and ring and little fingers in the other.

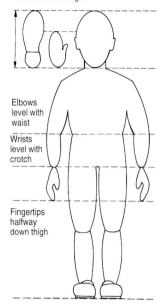

Hands reach from the chin to the middle of the forehead

Feet are a little larger

Elbows level with waist

Wrists level with crotch

Fingertips halfway down thigh

Fig 13 (a) Typical proportions for a puppet

Fig 12 The setting of the head on the neck has a significant influence on characterization

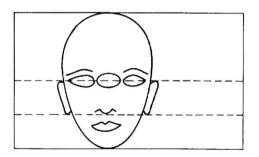

Fig 13 (b) suitable proportions for the head – top of ears aligns with eyes; bottom of ears aligns with nose; the eyes are approximately one eye's width apart

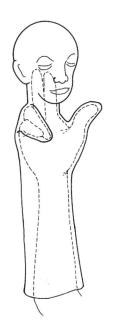

The puppet's hands may be made as part of the glove, separately in fabric, or sculpted, modelled or moulded, with a hollow wrist or cuff; its arms are attached securely to the cuff and the puppeteer's fingers are inserted to control the hands. This allows more character in the shape of the hands but more practice may be needed to achieve expressive gesture and to handle props effectively.

Glove puppets may be given legs. Carve, mould or model the foot and lower leg, and use a fabric thigh. Such legs usually swing freely; you can control them directly with the fingers of

Fig 14 (a) The basic glove puppet

Fig 16 Spotty Dog, an animal glove puppet in which the body effectively sits on the back of the operator's hand and wrist. Made from foam rubber, felt and fur fabric by Anna Braybrooke (now Anna Poland) for Polka Children's Theatre

Fig 15 Glove puppets may be given legs and feet, as with this Punch character cast in fibreglass by Geoff Felix for the Puppet Centre Collection. The mould was smashed to release the undercut rigid head. A plug with a two-finger space was cast to fit the neck for effective control

your free hand inserted into holes in the back of the thighs, but this limits you to operating only one puppet at a time.

For animal characters, make a simple glove with an animal head, covering the glove with a human costume, synthetic fur fabric, or other suitable material. Alternatively, a complete animal body that rests on the wrist and forearm may be made of cloth and stitched to the glove.

Hand Puppets

The term 'hand puppet' is used here to describe a puppet in which the operator's whole hand is inserted into the head. It usually has a moving mouth, operated with the thumb in the lower jaw. It may be a simple sleeve of material with a head attached, sometimes called a 'sleeve puppet', which is suit-

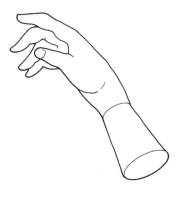

Fig 14 (b) A modelled hand with a hollow wrist

able both for human and animal characters. A stuffed body and dangling legs may be attached to the sleeve.

Two-handed puppets are made in the same way, leaving underneath a hole large enough to insert crossed arms; such a body is often stiffened by a buckram or foam-rubber lining.

If the hand puppet needs to maintain a rigid body shape, it may be made on a framework of strong card or wire netting (chicken wire), which is padded and covered.

A hand puppet may have a disproportionately large head and a very dominant mouth, hence its other name, 'mouth puppet'. One hand effects head, mouth and body movements. The puppeteer's other arm and hand are costumed. Alternatively, an additional operator may provide the puppet's hands. Puppet hands usually have only three fingers – two of the

operator's fingers are fitted into one of the puppet's – and this tends to look quite natural on the puppet.

Hand puppets tend to be large, so the head should be made of a light material, such as foam rubber or polystyrene, covered with fabric or synthetic fur fabric. The head is made with a separate lower jaw joined by a strong fabric hinge.

Make the body suitably full for the character. The whole puppet may be created in foam rubber, the head and a limb from blocks, and the body from sheet foam rubber.

Fig 18 A two-handed hand puppet

Fig 17 The crocodile from Punch and Judy is a form of 'sleeve puppet' with snappy wooden jaws padded with foam rubber and a long sleeve of fabric for the body

Fig 19 (a) A form of hand puppet, sometimes called a 'mouth puppet', with a gloved human hand. Created by Kumquats, Germany; available from the Puppet Centre;

Fig 19 (b) another view of the Kumquats puppet, showing the method of operation; black sleeves normally worn by the operator have been omitted for clarity

Rod Puppets

The body is designed to be supported by a central rod that is free to turn, but may be fixed if desired. Even a head and a robe with no body or limbs can be effective, and the natural movement of the fabric contributes to this. A rod puppet frequently has a head, shoulder block, arms, hands and robes, but no body or legs, as it is usually visible only to waist or hip level. If it has no body, appropriate padding under the costume assists characterization.

A short central rod gives more scope for movement, as the operator's wrist becomes the puppet's waist, but a long rod enables the puppet to be held much higher.

It is a simple matter to attach the head to the central rod to permit it to turn and look up and down. If it is only to turn, the head may be constructed with the neck attached, then secured on the central rod. The rod turns inside the shoulder block/body. If the head is to move vertically, construct it without a neck but with an elongated hole in its base; it pivots on the top of the central rod that forms the neck. A pull-string or a piece of stiff wire is then used to control vertical movement. The rod is also able to turn inside the shoulder block or body.

In each case, a supporting 'collar' is attached to the rod under the shoulder block or inside the body; this holds it in place on the rod, but permits turning.

Hand movement is effected by thin but stiff metal rods. If the puppet has legs, they usually swing loose; often, an additional puppeteer is needed if they are to be manipulated.

A rod puppet with a body and legs, plus robes and controls can be a considerable weight, so design the puppet and select construction materials and costume fabrics accordingly. The larger the puppet, the more important it is to use a material such as polystyrene rather than wood.

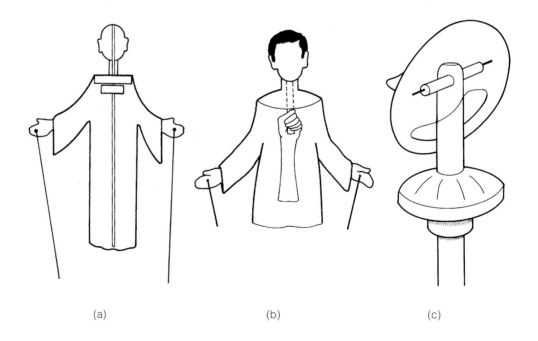

Fig 20 (a) A basic rod puppet with a shoulder block but no body or legs. The long rod enables it to be held high, but limits body movement;

Fig 20 (b) a short central rod limits the height of the puppet, but permits considerable scope for movement;

Fig 20 (c) for nodding, the head has an elongated hole in the base and pivots on the central rod

(a)   (b)   (c)

Fig 21 A rod puppet with legs: Lorenzo by Barry Smith for Theatre of Puppets' production of Keats' *Isabella* (or *The Pot of Basil*)

Fig 22 A rod puppet cat with a flexible body and moving eyes

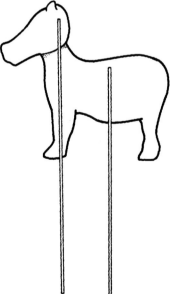

Fig 23 For an animal rod puppet, a rod to the body provides the main support while an additional rod controls head movements

Animal Rod Puppets

Animal puppets can be made from a wide variety of materials. Two common techniques are to build a head and body by one of the regular methods of modelling, moulding or sculpting, or to create a body around a central core of rope, spring, flexible tubing, and so on.

The head and body may be created as a single unit without a joint, but normally the head moves separately from the body, controlled by an extra rod directly to the head or inserted through the body. The supporting rod for the body is attached at a point suitable for good balance.

The legs may be made from jointed wood, laminated plywood shapes, or in a variety of creative ways (if the puppet is given legs at all).

Bunraku-Style Rod Puppets

The term *Bunraku* refers to a Japanese style of performance that is a blend of the arts of puppet theatre, narration and *samisen* music. The head of a true *Bunraku* puppet is carved and hollowed, sometimes with a range of moving features. It is mounted on a head-grip, which fits into a wooden shoulder board with padded ends.

Two strips of material hang from the shoulders at the front and back; to the

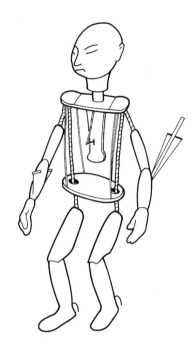

Fig 25 The structure of a *Bunraku* puppet

bottom of these is attached a bamboo hoop or a piece of wood for the hips. The limbs are carved, often with shaped and stuffed fabric upper parts; strings from the arms and legs are tied to the shoulder board. The padded costume creates the real body shape and character.

The chief operator inserts his left hand through a slit in the back of the costume and holds the head-grip to control head and body. With his right hand he moves the right arm. A toggle, pivoted in the arm and with strings attached, is used to effect hand movements. A second operator uses his right hand to move the puppet's left arm by means of a rod about 38cm (15in) long joined to the arm near the elbow. The hand is moved by two strings attached to a small crossbar on the rod; the operator uses his index and middle fingers hooked around these strings. The legs are moved by a third operator using

Fig 24 A *Bunraku* puppet

Fig 26 Pierrot: the main operator supports the body and controls the head with a short central rod, also operating the left arm through a long rod with a toggle control to effect hand movements. A second operator controls the right arm, and a third operator controls the legs and feet

Fig 27 Pierrot from *Pierrot in Five Masks* by Barry Smith's Theatre of Puppets. The puppet is operated in *Bunraku* style by three people. Different latex-rubber masks fit on to a covered polystyrene head shape

inverted L-shaped metal rods fixed just above the heel.

This technique has been adapted to a range of practices with one, two or three-person operation. The neck is often angled somewhat and the basic head-grip is made from a rod or a strong strip of plywood. If plywood is used, one end is built into the neck, and the other end is made into a pistol-grip handle by gluing on shaped pieces of wood.

The hand is attached to the arm with or without a flexible wrist joint. A control rod, operated from behind, is inserted into the heel of the hand or the

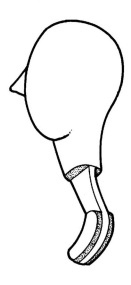

Fig 28 An angled neck
attached to a pistol-grip
control

arm at the elbow or wrist, as appropriate. The hand-control rod (which may be weighted if required) can act as a partial counterbalance to the arm, so that it does not hang lifeless by the puppet's side while it is not being operated. Toggle hand controls may be added.

Hand-Rod Puppets

This is a cross between a hand puppet and a rod puppet, usually with a moving mouth. The operator's hand is inserted for head, mouth and body movements; the hands and arms are controlled by rods.

Rod-Hand Puppets

This type of puppet requires one or two operators. At its simplest it has a central rod and a robe, but no body; usually it has at least shoulders to help establish body shape. The puppeteer holds the rod in one hand and uses the other hand, costumed, as the puppet's hand, or slips a gloved hand through a slit in the puppet's robe; the slit may be elasticated if desired. Alternatively, one puppeteer operates head and body and another provides the costumed hands and arms.

Fig 29 A hand-rod
puppet of the type used
for many Muppet
characters

Fig 30 A rod-hand puppet with a short central rod and shoulder block, but with gloved human hands

Rod-Glove Puppets

This puppet retains the directness and potential of the glove puppet yet has the stature and proportions of the rod puppet. The head is secured to a central rod but it has a glove-style body, to which are attached separate hands with tubular arms. The puppeteer moves the arms and hands with thumb and index finger, and holds the rod with the other fingers. The costume is attached to a small shoulder block that sits on a supporting collar.

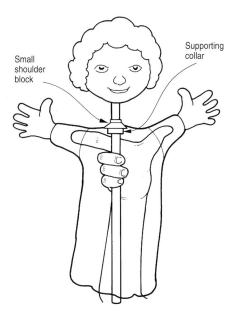

Fig 31 A rod-glove puppet has a smaller shoulder block sitting on the supporting collar

Rod-Marionettes

The term rod-marionette refers to various types of puppet operated from above, like marionettes, either by rods and strings, or just by rods. The traditional Sicilian puppets, carved in wood with beaten brass armour, are operated in this way by strong metal

Fig 32 A Sicilian rod-marionette used to perform many episodes of the story of *Orlando Furioso*

Fig 33 The Sicilian style of rod-marionette has been adapted for this character which has a modelled head: Ubu, from *Ubu Roi*, performed by Barry Smith's Theatre of Puppets

rods to the head and the sword arm, and a cord to the shield arm. Twisting the head-rod from side to side creates sufficient momentum to make the legs swing.

The same style is used for the puppet in Fig 33 while the animal in Fig 34 has head- and body-'rods', through which total control is effected. When the puppet is standing upright, its momentum and the gentle swaying of its body causes its hind legs to walk; when on all fours, walking is achieved by alternately lifting front and rear rods with slight forward pressure. To reduce the weight, the rods may be constructed from aluminium tube; the

Fig 34 Rod-marionette principles applied to an animal

puppet also needs to be made from a fairly lightweight material.

A rod-marionette of the type used in southern India, often called a 'body puppet', is suspended on strings attached to a cloth-bound ring on the puppeteer's head and controlled by the puppeteer's head movement and hand rods. The puppeteer's shoes may be attached to the puppet's feet too.

Marionettes

The essence of good marionette construction is balance and distribution of weight, coupled with flexibility of movement and joints restricted appropriately to allow adequate control. A well-made marionette moves in ways in which a poorly constructed marionette cannot. It is important, therefore, to design the marionette as a

Fig 35 'Body puppets' created by John Blundall for a production of *The Pomegranate Princess*

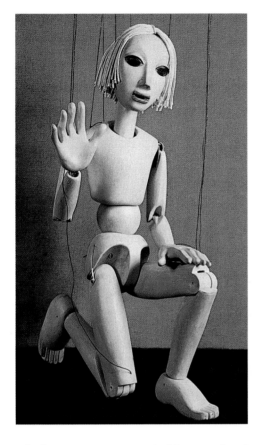

Fig 36 A beautiful wooden marionette carved by John Wright for the Puppet Centre Collection. The style and construction methods are typical of the marionettes created by Wright for productions at the Little Angel Theatre

Fig 37 Marionette parts in latex rubber ready for assembly

whole, to ensure a suitable match of materials that will provide the balance required. This is why heavy legs should not be attached to a light body, for example.

Few marionettes work as effectively as carved ones. The carved marionette in Fig 36 is perfectly constructed and moves as beautifully as it looks. If you do not have carving skills, you should not be discouraged, however: marionettes may be simple or complex, and there is an effective method at every level of ability.

Whatever the materials chosen, certain basic principles apply, as follows.

The head moves most effectively if it is made with the neck separate from both head and body. However, it may be made with the neck attached or, exceptionally, the neck may be made as

part of the body, and joined inside the head for a particular purpose. A body is normally jointed at the waist but its movement may be restricted as required. Making the body without a waist joint limits a puppet's movements, particularly its walk.

Hands and feet are best constructed in the same material as the head. Although the wrist joint is usually designed to allow flexibility, the ankle joint is somewhat restricted, to prevent the toes dragging as the puppet walks.

To achieve precise control it may be necessary to weight a puppet, although a well-made figure should not need it. It is important that the pelvis is not too light as this will affect the puppet's walking action. If it is necessary to weight the foot, avoid making the toe

Fig 38 Muffin the Mule.
This larger version (now in
the Puppet Centre Hogarth
Collection) of the television
original was made for
Muffin's first live
performance in
pantomime. The structure
of this carved puppet is
typical of many animal
marionettes

too heavy or it will drag when walk-ing. The usual method for adding weight is to glue or nail on a piece of sheet lead (available from builders' merchants). When parts are cast in rubber, pour liquid plaster into the part to be weighted.

Most controls require two-handed operation – an upright control is rec-ommended for 'human' characters, and a horizontal (or 'aeroplane') control for animals. Some have the walking action built into the main control, while oth-ers have a separate leg-bar, which is preferable for 'humans'.

Animal Marionettes

Heads and bodies for animals are made from a variety of materials (*see* Chapter 3). Legs are usually carved or created with laminated layers of plywood; these may be further shaped with a modelling material, or padded to shape with foam rubber if the leg is to be cov-ered with fabric. Feet may be carved or made from the same material as the head. A form of horizontal control is appropriate for most animals. (For the basic structure for most animals, *see* Fig 38.)

3 Heads – Materials and Methods

A variety of materials, and techniques – sculpting, modelling and casting – may be used for making the head of a puppet. Before you start to make a head, however, you should plan the entire puppet, construction methods and joints to be used, and, particularly, decide whether the head should be made with or without a neck attached.

TOOLS

An effective puppet workshop needs a small collection of tools. Care should be taken for reasons of safety, and out of respect for your tools: a chisel used to open paint tins will have a short life as a woodworking tool, and brushes quickly need to be replaced if they are not cleaned properly. Keep scissors sharp by using them only for particular materials; don't use your fabric scissors for cutting card, and so on.

For those embarking upon wood-carving, proper wood-carving tools are recommended; they can be very expensive, but the beginner should be able to find a set of basic tools that is reasonably priced.

Fig 39 Characters designed and made from wood and fabric by John Blundall for a production of *Giants, Witches and Fighting Men* by Dave Arthur

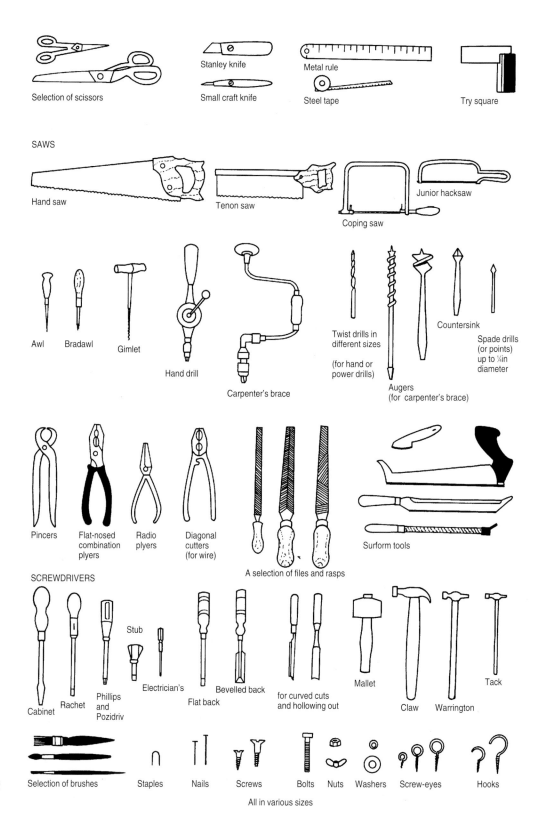

Selection of scissors

Stanley knife

Small craft knife

Metal rule

Steel tape

Try square

SAWS

Hand saw

Tenon saw

Coping saw

Junior hacksaw

Awl   Bradawl   Gimlet

Hand drill

Carpenter's brace

Twist drills in different sizes

(for hand or power drills)

Augers
(for carpenter's brace)

Countersink

Spade drills (or points) up to ¼in diameter

Pincers   Flat-nosed combination plyers   Radio plyers   Diagonal cutters (for wire)

A selection of files and rasps

Surform tools

SCREWDRIVERS

Stub

Electrician's

Cabinet   Rachet   Phillips and Pozidriv

Flat back   Bevelled back

for curved cuts and hollowing out

Mallet

Claw   Warrington   Tack

Selection of brushes   Staples   Nails   Screws   Bolts   Nuts   Washers   Screw-eyes   Hooks

All in various sizes

Fig 40 A useful selection of tools

EXPLORING MATERIALS

Some materials may prove frustrating to work with until you have mastered the medium, but do persevere. Explore a range of materials and give each one a reasonable try. As new materials appear, explore their potential. They need to be flexible in their application, easily modelled, cast or sculpted, lightweight but strong and durable, not prone to chipping or cracking, nor to shrinking excessively or distorting when drying, easily cut with appropriate tools when dry, and amenable to use with a variety of paints and adhesives.

Some materials frequently used for puppet-making have been re-formulated in order to prevent substance abuse and remove other health hazards. This has changed their properties and made them unsuitable for modelling, so take care about following advice in old books.

SCULPTING

General Principles

When sculpting, you start with a block, visualize what you want to achieve, and have to know what to cut away and what to leave. (Of course, with some materials it is easy to glue pieces back on if you cut away too much.)

Do not make the profile too flat, particularly the back of the head; you usually need a greater distance from the back to the front of the head than from side to side. For the key stages in developing a head, *see* Fig 41. With all sculpting methods, any outlines drawn on the block will be lost as the work progresses, so keep re-drawing these as necessary.

Sculpted heads are usually made from foam rubber, polystyrene, or

wood but builders' expanding foam filler has recently emerged as a useful medium.

Foam Rubber

Foam-rubber heads are quickly made and tend to be used for large figures such as mouth puppets. Foam rubber is usually covered with a suitable fabric as it discolours or fades over time. It is not very suitable for marionette heads.

Upholstery foam is the preferred type; use good-quality foam, or it may crumble with age. It is quite a tough material to cut; suitable tools are a bread knife (preferably electric), a hacksaw blade, a craft knife, or very sharp scissors. For a smooth finish, use a small Surform rasp. Also use a suitable adhesive; electric glue guns are excellent, but take care as hot glue can cause severe burns.

Fig 41 The main stages in sculpting a head

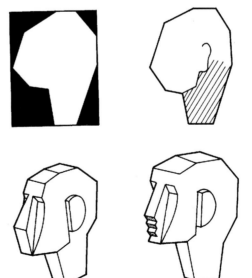
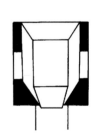
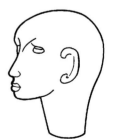

Fig 42 Orm, a hand puppet worm made for television by Mary Edwards. The head and torso are made from sculpted foam, the tail from wire rings with polyester filling and stretch cotton-knit fabric

Fig 43 Gas Cat, a very large hand puppet with a modelled fibreglass skull (to accomodate a mechanism for moving eyes), covered with sculpted foam and fur fabric. It has a moving mouth and the eyes are spring-loaded, with a control string for sideways movement. The hands are operated by a second puppeteer. Made for a television commercial by Mary Edwards

First sketch the outline and essential features full-face and in profile on the block. (If using a felt pen, beware of it rubbing off on your clothes.) Establish the basic shape with an electric bread knife (or other appropriate tool), then shape detail with scissors and a sharp knife, finishing with a rasp. For a rugged finish, pull pieces of foam from the block. If you cut away too much, or to add features, glue on pieces of foam. To open deep holes, for rods or other internal fixtures, use a thin, long, coarse and raspy round file.

For the eyes, you can carve out sockets and glue in large painted wooden balls. It is possible to hollow the head to install moving eyes, but foam can cling and impede movement; other materials are more suitable for a head incorporating such a feature – the basic skull shape could be created in fibreglass to accommodate the eyes and eye mechanism, then covered in foam rubber sculpted to the precise shape.

Foam rubber is usually covered with a suitably textured fabric: towelling, lycra, stretchy cottons and synthetic fur fabric are common. Try to minimize the number of joins and to arrange them so they will be least noticeable. Depending on the needs of the situation and the fabric used, the covering may be attached to the foam with an appropriate adhesive, either at key points or all over. Alternatively, the fabric covering may be stretched and stitched securely over the foam structure. Some makers stitch the panels with a castellated (not zig-zag) stitch, to pull the fabric seams together cleanly and tightly.

If necessary, paint and finish the head (*see* page 43).

Polystyrene

Polystyrene (Styrofoam) is an excellent, very light medium. Because blocks are shaped by melting or cutting, make sure you use fire-resistant polystyrene and ensure good ventilation. Large off-cuts from packaging or display-making firms are ideal.

Establish the basic shape with a rasp, a hand saw, a hacksaw blade, a heat gun or any hot implement. (Rasps and blades are preferable because of the fumes caused by heating.) Deep modelling is necessary or detail will be lost when the head is covered. You cannot carve fine details in polystyrene, but you can refine your basic shaping, with coarse and then with fine glasspaper. Before covering the head, add detail or accentuate features with pieces of string, cord, or other suitable materials.

Cover the surface of the polystyrene with small pieces of strong brown paper or muslin, using pearl glue. To do this, first coat the head in glue, soak the paper or muslin in the glue and then cover the head with it, overlapping the pieces and smoothing each piece very carefully. Three layers should be sufficient; allow each layer to dry before applying the next. Change the colour of each layer to ensure full

Fig 44 Angelo and Angelina from *Angelo*, a Little Angel Theatre production with puppets made by Lyndie Wright. The design was based upon illustrations by Quentin Blake, and the characters sculpted in polystyrene and covered with paper, gesso (gypsum) and plaster filler, and emulsion paint, before final painting

coverage of the head. If the neck is to be hollow, line it with glue and paper or muslin. Some makers cover the last layer of paper with a coat of glue, then sand it lightly, before painting.

Note: Many glues dissolve polystyrene, so use pearl glue or a contact adhesive produced specifically for expanded polystyrene.

Expanding Foam Filler

Note: Use foam filler in well-ventilated conditions and away from sources of ignition, and wear protective gloves when initially extruding it.

Builders' expanding foam filler is an aerosol-applied filler which expands and cures on contact with moisture. It does not adhere to plastic or polythene sheeting, or to clingfilm, and may be released from other materials by using a suitable agent such as silicone jelly. It expands up to two and a half times its volume, so do not extrude too

Fig 45 (a) Extruding expanding foam filler into a container to create a block for later sculpting;

Fig 45 (b) when set, the block is removed from the container. It adheres strongly to the central dowel, which can be used for securing to a marionette body or for a rod-puppet control

much. If it does not expand sufficiently, spray with water and add more foam. It may remain soggy or tacky if there is not enough water, or if it is in a closed container.

When the foam filler has cured, it may be sanded or cut to shape as required and is easier to shape than polystyrene; a bread knife is especially useful for shaping large blocks. You can either spray the foam on to a basic shape, and refine the shaping when the foam is fully expanded and cured, or you can create a block of foam of a particular size for sculpting.

If you are building on a basic shape, spray it with water before adding the foam.

To make a block for sculpting, use a suitably shaped container with a large open end; a plastic margarine box is ideal. Spray the inside with water, squirt in the foam filler to the deepest parts of the box, and allow it to expand. To maximize expansion, fill to a depth of about 25mm (1in), spray with water, then add another 25mm layer and continue until the container is about forty per cent full. If the head needs an internal rod, ensure it is held securely in the box and spray it with water before squirting in the foam filler; the foam will expand around it. When the foam has fully expanded and cured (a 25mm layer of filler will be ready to work on in two hours), prise it out of the plastic tub, or break the tub away if it is no longer needed.

Whichever method is used, shape the head and cover with a finishing layer of an appropriate material (*see* page 31). If you cut away too much in sculpting, spray with water and squirt on a little extra foam filler, then shape again.

To glue together two pieces, trim one surface to expose the open cell structure (removing any skin-like finish),

spray both surfaces with water and use a gap-filling adhesive.

Applicator nozzles and tubes may be cleaned in acetone or toluene while the filler is still soft. If the filler sets hard in the tube, flex the tube to separate it from the filler and poke out the filler. The instructions recommend plugging the valve of the can with a moistened matchstick, but take care how you remove it: a good clean pull with a pair of pliers should remove the matchstick, together with any solid filler in the valve, but if the matchstick breaks off, you will have problems re-using the can.

Wood

Wood-carving is a sophisticated art but many puppeteers with no special training make beautiful carved heads, having developed their own individual techniques. Surform rasps can be used for general shaping – they are efficient tools, easy to use and very safe – and with some woods a considerable amount of modelling may be done with glasspaper.

A small selection of wood-working chisels is useful. The late John Wright (*Rod, Shadow and Glove Puppets at the Little Angel Theatre*, Hale, 1986) recommended as a starter set a 16mm and a 25mm flat chisel, a 6mm fishtail flat, a 6mm deep gouge and a 13mm shallow gouge, plus a wood-carving mallet and a pair of callipers for comparing measurements. A set of wood-carving tools, properly used, is a considerable asset. You also need a sharpening stone and oil, and a strong rigid workbench or table with a wooden vice (metal jaws must be padded with wood). Powered bandsaws are also useful for cutting basic shapes.

Use a well-seasoned close-grained hardwood. Limewood is recommended; easily worked, it does not splinter readily and is quite light in weight. American whitewood has similar qualities, but lime is preferable. Jelutong, a Malaysian wood, is popular for larger puppet parts and simple heads. It is not suitable for those with thin or delicate parts, but different woods can be joined together, for example, using oak for parts that need to withstand harsh treatment. Select the wood carefully in a suitable size; avoid pieces with cracks, stains and knots, and look for a straight grain. For limewood you might need a specialist timber merchant.

Remember the head is much deeper than it is wide, so allow plenty of wood for the front to back dimension. Join two pieces with wood-working adhesive if necessary.

When carving for the first time, practise on spare pieces of the type of wood to be used, then tackle the body and limbs before carving the feet and hands, and lastly the head. Use the wood so that the grain runs vertically down through the whole puppet (except the feet), and make chisel cuts in the same direction as the grain; otherwise, the wood will split and vital parts of the figure will be lost.

Strike the chisel with firm, sharp taps of the mallet rather than heavy blows. For fine paring, hold the chisel with the end of the shaft in the palm of one hand, against the heel, and the other hand over the shaft and blade, helping to guide it. Always keep both hands behind the direction of the cutting edge. Occasionally sand the surface to study progress and re-draw outlines that are lost as the carving proceeds.

Carve the face and front half of the head, back almost as far as the ears,

Fig 46 One of the Kings, designed by Lyndie Wright and carved in wood by John Wright for the Little Angel Theatre production of the operetta, *Amahl and the Night Visitors* by Menotti

Fig 47 The late John Wright, OBE, carving in the workshop of the Little Angel Theatre. Note the block of wood screwed to the head for holding in the vice for carving, and the method for holding the chisel

holding the other half of the block firmly in the vice. Remove the major part of the waste with a saw and chisel, then establish the actual shape with chisels.

Sand to a smooth finish, starting with coarse glasspaper on the roughest parts and working down to a very fine paper. When the face is complete, work towards the back of the head, leaving blocks for the ears so that the head can continue to be held in the vice. Finally, carefully shape the ears and hollow out the socket for the neck and as much of the head as possible through this hole, to reduce weight.

Another method is to screw a block of wood securely to the bottom of the head and to hold this block in the vice, removing it when no longer needed.

MODELLING

General Principles

Modelling allows you to establish the basic structure in the model upon which you make the head, and then to use a chosen material to build up the

features until the desired effect is achieved. Some materials permit you to cut away during modelling or when the head is dry. Most modelling materials, used in an appropriate thickness, are both strong and reasonably light-weight.

Be aware of the difference in spatial orientation of puppet to maker and puppet to audience, particularly for rod and glove puppets. Do not angle the puppet head upwards, or its focus will be above the audience. You might tilt it slightly forwards, but not too noticeably. Lift the modelling stand occasionally and view the puppet from the angle of the audience.

For a glove puppet, you could line the inside and edge of the neck with fabric to improve the operator's comfort.

MODELLING ON PLASTICINE

Make a modelling stand of suitable proportions by screwing together a dowel and a block of wood. Model the basic head shape in plasticine (plastilene) around the dowel, avoiding fine detail. Alternative modelling materials

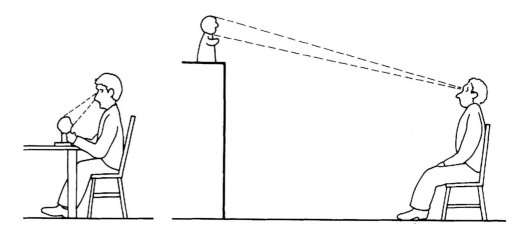

Fig 48 The relationship of puppet to maker and puppet to audience

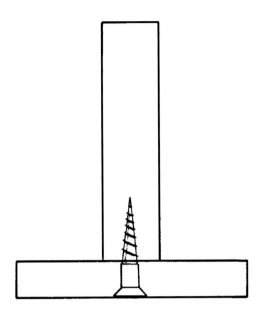

Fig 49 A modelling stand

Hold the shells up to the light to test for weak points that may need strengthening; these are commonly found under the nose and around the eyes. Remove any trace of separator before applying modelling material to the inside of the head. At this stage, complete any internal mechanisms and re-join the shells.

MODELLING UPON A BASE SHAPE

You may model upon any suitably shaped object (for example, an egg-shaped piece of polystyrene, or a shape created in cardboard), which may either remain inside, or be removed from, the hardened shell. Either fix the shape on to a modelling stand and model upon it, or work on it hand-held; either way, ensure that you can stand it or hang it up to dry. When the head is complete, leave the base shape in the head or, if you are using polystyrene, you may scoop it out or dissolve it with a few drops of acetone.

A cardboard base shape is extremely strong and, like polystyrene, useful for larger puppets. Draw the profile shape on strong cardboard and cut it out. If any internal fixture is required, such as dowelling for securing the neck, glue it in place and build the head around it. Glue on cardboard 'ribs' to create the head shape. Strengthen the ribs with strips of cardboard glued between them. If moving eyes or mouth are required, cut away the cardboard as necessary to accommodate these.

Cover the structure with layers of thin card, then cover the cardboard with a thin layer of the desired modelling material and build up detail as required. With some materials it is helpful to smear the card with a suitable glue before modelling. Alternatively, you can cover the card with cloth or synthetic fur fabric.

Fig 50 Modelling upon a base shape:

Fig 50 (a) a cardboard profile shape with 'ribs' glued on;

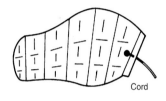
Cord

Fig 50 (b) braces glued between the ribs;

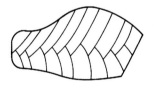

Fig 50 (c) the shape covered with strips of thin card

may be used for the basic shape, but do use one that remains pliable rather than one that sets hard, or it will be difficult to remove from the head at a later stage.

Cut out cardboard ears and insert them into the plasticine for a good base on which to build. Where necessary, apply a coating of a suitable 'release agent' or separator to the head (but not the ears), then cover it with a modelling material which dries to form a hard shell. Cut the head open (behind the ears and in a V-shape on top of the head, to aid alignment when re-joining) and remove the plasticine.

If the head does not separate cleanly from the plasticine when it is cut in two, slice through the plasticine with strong, fine thread or wire to separate the front and back sections. Carefully scoop out some of the central plasticine with a spoon and roll the plasticine away from the shell into this space. Never apply leverage against the head shell.

Fig 51 (a) A plasticine model with cardboard ears;

Fig 51 (b) overlapping squares of paper pasted to the head;

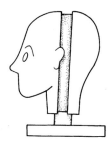

Fig 51 (c) when dry, the head is cut open and the plasticine removed

Paste and Paper

Create a plasticine model with cardboard ear shapes. Cover the plasticine, but not the cardboard, with overlapping 25mm (1in) squares of damp tissue paper, to prevent the head shell sticking to the plasticine.

Apply to the head, including the ears, at least four layers of newspaper in small squares using PVA glue or a cellular paste. Alternate the colour of the layers to ensure full coverage. Work in detail (but keeping it bold) with tissue paper – it is more easily modelled – and then continue covering with newspaper. If you are using cellular paste, let each layer dry before applying the next.

When the modelling is complete and thoroughly dry, cut it open and remove the plasticine. If any internal structure is needed, such as a dowel for securing head strings for a marionette, insert it now. Finally, re-join the shells with paste and paper.

Paper Pulp

Soak small pieces of newspaper in water until it turns to pulp (use a food processor to speed this up), drain off excess water and add powder paste

Fig 52 A head made from layers of paste and paper. Note also the wig, made from white parcel cord wound around drinking straws covered in glue

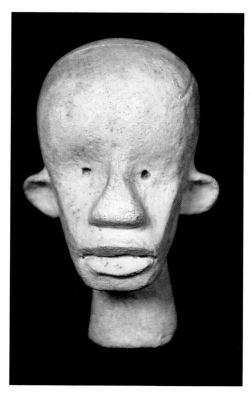

Fig 53 A head made from paper pulp mixed with sawdust, by Barry Smith

and water to arrive at a porridge-like consistency. Some makers also mix in very fine sawdust.

Create a plasticine base shape on a modelling stand and cover with squares of damp tissue paper as a separator. Model the pulp on to this. When dry, cut it open, remove the core, then re-join with glue and pulp. Sand it lightly and fill any cracks with pulp.

Plaster and Muslin

This is essentially the same technique as paste and paper. The modelling for such features as eye sockets must be deep, as they will tend to flatten out as the material is applied.

Cover a modelled head with damp tissue paper and apply overlapping squares of muslin (mull) dipped in plaster filler. Alternatively, use Mod-rock, a cotton bandage impregnated with plaster, similar to that used for setting broken limbs. Simply dip the Mod-rock into water and apply it immediately.

Apply at least three layers, pressing each one firmly into the previous one. There is no need to wait for one layer to dry before applying the next. Colour alternate layers with paint to ensure full coverage.

Build detail with finely teased cotton wool saturated in plaster filler. When dry, this may be shaped with a craft knife or glasspaper.

When it is thoroughly dry, cut open the head, remove the plasticine and strengthen the shell if necessary. Re-join and cover the head with another layer of muslin. For a very smooth finish, apply enough filler to fill the texture of the muslin and smooth it with a wet finger. If you use too much, it may chip in use. Sand lightly with fine glasspaper if required.

Milliput (Epoxy Putty)

Milliput is the trade name for an epoxy putty, produced in different grades. Standard Yellow/Grey is satisfactory for puppets, but finer grades are available. It sets rock hard, but can be cut, drilled and sanded just like wood. Used extensively by model-makers for some time, it has only recently become more widely used by puppeteers. Although there is not a long history of use with puppets, experience to date suggests that it is a very appropriate material, even though a little initial mixing is needed.

Each pack contains two sticks of the substance, which is rather like plasticine to handle. The soft putty needs to be mixed together until all streaks have disappeared, when it becomes very adhesive and at room temperature sets rock hard, without shrinking, in two to three hours. Setting time can be reduced to a few minutes by heating. It is fully cured at the same temperature over a period equivalent to the setting time. After curing it can be worked – drilled, cut, filed, sanded or painted – immediately.

Milliput adheres well to itself (and to many other materials), so it is easy to add detail after it has set. It responds well to water, which aids manipulation and smoothing; you can even smooth the surface under a running tap or with wet fingers while it is still soft. Keep fingers and tools moist to prevent sticking, and clean tools immediately after use with a wet rag or paper. Once Milliput has hardened, it is almost impossible to remove.

Because of this material's adhesive properties, you might prefer to model directly upon a shape such as polystyrene, which may be left in the head or dissolved out. Work details with modelling tools or other appropriate implements. With some base shape materials you will need to use a release agent such as Ambersil DP100/2, a silicone spray, or petroleum jelly.

If modelling upon plasticine, you should not need a separator; normally the plasticine will simply peel away from the Milliput, but try a test piece first and, if necessary, apply a release agent. When the shell is dry, saw it open and remove the plasticine. Complete any internal mechanisms, re-join the two shells, and cover the joint with the putty.

Alternatively, use Milliput to create a basic head shape, like a hollow egg or sphere, then model all the features solidly once the hollowed shell is re-joined.

Fibreglass

Fibreglass is not a pleasant medium with which to work, but it suits some people and some applications (*see* Fig 15). Fibreglass matting is supplied in various grades and is used with poly-ester liquid resin. The use of rubber gloves is recommended.

Cover the base model with damp tissue paper before applying fibreglass. Saturate pieces of the matting in the liquid resin, press out all bubbles and then press the matting on to the model with the pieces overlapping. Use 'finishing matt' for the first layer if the inside of the head needs to be smooth (for glove puppets, or where you have moving eyes or mouth). Build up the head and features in coarse matt, then apply a final layer of fine-quality matt.

To remove the core, cut open the head with a sharp knife before it is completely hard. If it hardens, a saw will be needed to cut it. Join the shells with saturated matting and sand the head (you can also file it if necessary).

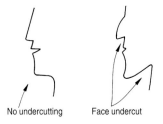

No undercutting   Face undercut

Fig 54 The face on the left has no under-cutting, but the one on the right is under-cut

CASTING

General Principles

Casting (or moulding) involves taking a plaster cast of a model and using the cast to make copies in the chosen material. You can get the finished product exactly right in the initial plasticine model and you can renew heads easily. You can make identical heads for a character in different costumes, or for one that appears as a rod puppet, a glove puppet and a marionette, or for family members, with appropriate finishing touches.

Heads can be created in a range of materials using this technique. When using materials that dry rigid, under-cutting is not possible without smashing the plaster to remove the head. However, the flexibility of latex rubber (provided it is not allowed to become too thick) does permit under-cutting.

Some latex mixes and fibreglass can shrink by as much as ten per cent compared with the original model. To allow for shrinkage, create the basic shape to the required size in poly-styrene, then finish the modelling with a covering of plasticine up to 10mm (⅜in) thick. When the plaster cast is complete, dissolve the polystyrene with acetone, remove the plasticine and proceed as usual. Experimentation is needed to determine the thickness of the plasticine in relation to the size of head and material used for the final product.

Making a Plaster Cast

You can make the cast from plaster of Paris, but quick-setting 'stonehard' dental plaster is far superior. You must work quickly once it starts to set, but it dries out ready for use in a very short time and is remarkably strong. When mixing the plaster, add the powder to the water, fairly thinly at first. A chemical reaction takes place and it will thicken very quickly, feeling warm to the touch as it does so. Always ensure that you have mixed enough, and waste a little rather than having to start over.

Two techniques are favoured: the hand-held method for the application of plaster is suitable for moderate-sized heads and is more economical on plaster; the box method is better for larger heads that are not easily worked using the hand-held method.

THE HAND-HELD METHOD

If it is to be a rigid head, insert thin strips of metal (for example, tin) into the plasticine model, over the head and down the sides across the line of the ears. For a flexible latex head, insert the metal strips around the back of the head under the hairline: the head can be manoeuvred out of the cast and this avoids an unsightly flash down the ears and neck. Overlap the strips by 3-4mm (⅛in) to form a secure division between the front and back of the head. Smear the plasticine and the metal strips with petroleum jelly.

Mix the plaster in accordance with the manufacturer's instructions. Hold the back of the head in one hand and work on the front half. As soon as the plaster starts to thicken, scoop it up with a spoon and fill in all the hollows; some will run off, but keep applying it. As the plaster turns creamy, pour it all over this half of the head. The plaster should be 30-50mm (1-2in) thick.

Allow this cast to harden for about thirty minutes, then carefully remove the metal strips with tweezers and smooth any marks made by the dividers. Make a few shallow holes in the clean edge left by removing the metal strips. Smear the edge of the cast,

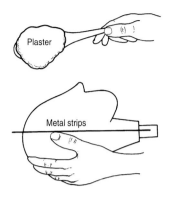

Fig 56 (a) Making the front section of the plaster cast;

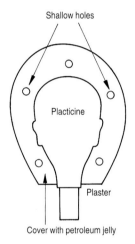

Fig 56 (b) making the back section of the cast

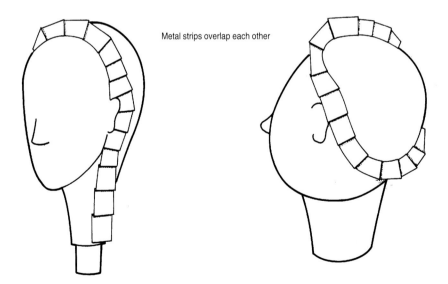

Metal strips overlap each other

Fig 55 Making a plaster cast using the hand-held method – (a) the plasticine model with metal dividing strips inserted for casting;

Fig 55 (b) dividing the plasticine model within the hairline including the shallow holes, with petroleum jelly, ensuring there are no lumps of grease, especially in the holes. Now take a cast of the back of the head. As it sets, carefully scrape away any excess plaster that overlaps the first cast.

When the cast is hard, prise the two sections apart and remove the plasticine. The back section of the cast will have knobs around the edge to fit into the holes in the front section. This allows the two shells to be aligned accurately for casting a rubber head.

Clean the inside of the cast carefully with a rag soaked in methylated spirit (wood alcohol). Clean the ears, nose and other awkward cracks with loops of fine wire. If there are any little holes on the inside surface, caused by air bubbles, these will cause wart-like lumps on the puppet, so mix up a little extra plaster to fill them and smooth them off very carefully.

Leave the cast to dry out until it no longer feels cold and heavy.

THE BOX METHOD

Make the plasticine model on a modelling stand. For casting, replace the base of the modelling stand with a larger board; ensure the head is held securely. Roll out a long strip of plasticine, approximately 5cm (2in) wide and 12mm (½in) thick; ensure it has a neat edge, and use this to divide the head in two. Press it into place firmly, but take care not to spoil the modelling. Build out the corners and trim this divider into a rectangular shape. Smear the back of the head and the divider with petroleum jelly.

Create a box around the back of the head with a folded piece of strong card; seal the edges of the card with fairly large strips of plasticine, to ensure that

Fig 57 Making a plaster cast using the box method – (a) dividing the head with plasticine;

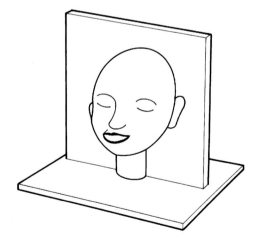

Fig 57 (b) the divider trimmed into a rectangle;

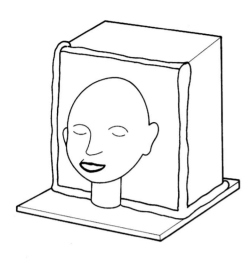

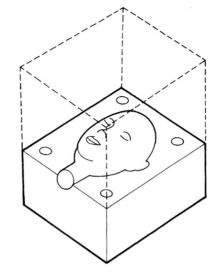

Fig 57 (c) a box created to contain the plaster;

Fig 57 (e) making the box to cast the front of the head

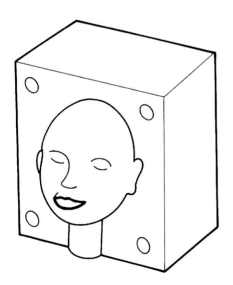

Fig 57 (d) the back section of the cast with holes scooped out;

the plaster cannot leak out and the box does not collapse.

Mix the plaster. As soon as it starts to thicken, pour it steadily into the box, gently shaking the board with your free hand in order to release any trapped air bubbles.

When the plaster has set, carefully remove the card and the divider and attend to any marks made on the head by the divider. Scoop shallow holes in the inside edge of the plaster block, and smear the front of the head and this edge of the block, including the shallow holes, with petroleum jelly.

Arrange the block so that the head is face upwards and fix another piece of folded card around it to box in the front of the head. Secure the card with plasticine and pour in the plaster, gently shaking the model, as before.

When the second half of the cast is set, remove the card, scrape away any surplus plaster covering the join, and carefully prise the two blocks apart. Finally, remove the plasticine, clean the cast and allow to dry.

Casting a Rigid Head

Most of the materials detailed for modelled heads, as well as expanding foam filler, can be used with plaster casts, but they all need a separator to prevent them sticking to the cast.

For paste and paper or paper pulp, use damp tissue paper or petroleum jelly (this must be cleaned off the head with methylated spirits before finishing and painting). For Milliput and expanding foam filler, use a silicone spray such as Ambersil DP100/2, and be sure to cover the edges of the cast too; for the filler, you could line the cast with clingfilm, provided it is pressed firmly into the surface. For fibreglass, a special separator is manufactured.

Fig 58 A head cast in latex with a hardener added. The puppet is by Barry Smith for Theatre of Puppets' production of *Isabella*

With modelling materials, cast each half of the head separately by pressing the material firmly into the casts, in accordance with the directions for use given on pages 36–38. When dry, the two shells are joined in the same way as a modelled head.

If you are using expanding foam filler (*see* Sculpting, page 31), be sure to spray the inside of the cast with water to facilitate curing, and take care to avoid air pockets as the foam expands but does not 'flow'. You must squirt the filler into the furthest chambers and all nooks and crannies. When set and cured, slice off the expanded foam flush with the cast; join the two sections by wetting both surfaces and applying gap-filling adhesive. Finally, apply a covering layer of a suitable material as described previously.

Some puppeteers add a hardener to latex rubber, described below, to make it rigid, but this removes the possibility of under-cutting and can make the head rather fragile.

Casting a Latex-Rubber Head

Latex rubber is obtained in a liquid state, with different colours, qualities and types of mix available. Most puppeteers use a fairly strong, soft-toy mix, or a grade used for hard rubber toys. These are sometimes identified by the numbers A360W or A443W (W is white, which is best as a base for colouring or painting). A330 may be too flexible for some purposes. Different grades can be mixed in varying proportions. You might wish to colour the latex before use; *see* page 43.

The larger the head, the thicker it needs to be in order to retain its shape. Large heads can be very heavy, so it is better to make them thinner, with some form of internal support. You can glue to the inside of the head a layer of foam rubber of appropriate thickness, or treat the latex-rubber head as a mask, and attach it to a skull shape created in foam rubber or polystyrene. Avoid stiffening any areas that are required to be flexible.

Secure the two parts of the cast together with strong rubber bands and/or cord; cover the join with plasticine. Pour the rubber carefully into the cast through the neck on to the inside surface, not directly into the centre and not from a great height, thus minimizing the occurrence of air bubbles. When it is approximately one-quarter full, roll the cast and tap it gently to fill in all the hollows and remove air bubbles; keep rolling it as you continue to fill it.

Top up the level of the rubber as it drops slightly. It will form a skin on the inside surface of the cast. The longer the rubber is left in the cast, the thicker this skin will be. Forty-five minutes to an hour will usually be sufficient, but it does depend on the rubber mix and how thick you want the head to be. Some experimentation may be necessary at first.

At the end of the required time, pour the excess rubber in the centre of the cast back into the container, to be used again. Leave the rubber in the cast to dry. Twenty-four hours is usually enough, but it depends on the thickness of the rubber, so be careful not to open the cast before the rubber is really dry.

Put a little talcum powder in the head, through the neck, and blow it around inside. This prevents the inner surfaces of the rubber sticking together. Prise the plaster cast apart and remove the head. If there is a 'flash', or ridge, around the head from the join in the cast, trim it off with a pair of sharp scissors.

Allow the head to dry for at least another twenty-four hours before painting it.

Fig 59 A cast in quick-setting 'stonehard' plaster, opened to reveal a latex head

PAINTING AND FINISHING HEAD, HANDS AND FEET

Principles for Painting the Face

Painting should not be undertaken until the necessary joints have been completed. In order to match skin tones, paint the head, hands and feet (if bare) all at the same time.

Natural colour tends to detract from the modelling and its dramatic effect, so consider the face in terms of stage make-up and lighting. Hansjurgen Fettig (*Glove and Rod Puppets*, Harrap, 1973) provides a particularly good discussion of colouring principles, which are included in the description below.

Fig 60 The main areas of light and shade on the face under typical stage lighting

Study each head under stage lighting before painting it, then paint in daylight, to see the true colours you are applying. Finally, check the finished product under coloured stage lighting again.

For an illustration of the major areas of light and shade of the face under typical stage lighting, *see* Fig 60. As a rule, forward-facing and protruding parts of the face appear lightest, side areas are lightly shaded, and recesses are in heavy shadow. Therefore, painting the protruding parts too dark or the shaded areas too light will neutralize the effect of the modelling and detract from the puppet's character.

Fettig suggests the use of four main shades: an overall application of a fairly light shade of the basic colour; a darker shade (of the same colour or appropriate other colour), applied to the areas of light shadow; a darker shade again for the recesses; and a very light shade for the frontal areas and protruding highlights.

Take account also of the space values and intensities of different colours. Warm colours appear nearer than cold colours, and stronger colours draw attention to themselves with a foreground appearance; pale colours, and those mixed with white, black or grey, tend to have a background quality.

Consideration of these principles leads to painting with good dramatic effect and will help you modify somewhat the apparent structure of a face; this is useful for disguising modelling weaknesses or creating different appearances from identical faces.

Materials and Methods

First apply a thin undercoat – white emulsion paint is quite suitable – and remember that carved wood will need priming first. Avoid leaving brush marks on the puppet, and ensure there are no thick blobs of paint in any hollows. The undercoat may be lightly sanded and another coat applied to achieve a fine, smooth finish on which to paint.

Whatever paint is used, avoid a glossy finish. Shiny faces and hands do not look convincing and they glare under lighting. If you cannot avoid a shiny finish, try dusting it lightly with talcum powder just before it dries. Shake, and then blow, the surplus from the head, then dust off the remainder with a *very* soft 6-12mm paintbrush. Continue to add powder and dust off as necessary, but take care not to smudge the paint.

For most needs, acrylic paints such as Reeves Polymer Colours, Rowney Cryla Colour or Liquitex are recommended. Mixed with water, they produce a good matt finish; painting on certain materials will require you to mix the paint with a medium, so select acrylic matt medium or it will dry slightly shiny. If you need to mix large quantities of colours which require a lot of white paint, white emulsion is a cheap substitute for an acrylic paint.

On fibreglass you will need to use polyurethane paints.

A range of techniques has evolved for the painting of latex-rubber heads. Some practitioners suggest colouring the latex with special rubber dyes, small quantities of thick emulsion paints, or aniline dyes. Mary Edwards of The Puppet Factory (*Workbench* in *Animations*, Yr 20, No. 4, 1997, Puppet Centre Ltd) recommends giving the latex a base colour before use. Use a small quantity of latex as a test; add liquid acrylic paints and note the proportions used (bear in mind that it dries darker). Aim for an undercoat shade rather than the actual skin tone. When the required colour is achieved, mix the quantity required in the same proportions. Add the paint carefully, to minimize air bubbles in the latex, then before use allow it to stand for a day in a sealed container, to allow any bubbles to disperse.

For the actual painting of a latex-rubber head, the paint needs some form of medium and should not be too thick, or it may crack as the rubber flexes. Mix the acrylic colour with the acrylic matt medium, or mix it with water and add *just a little* medium. Alternatively, liquid acrylic paints may be mixed with liquid latex in equal proportions, or with white wood-workers' glue (PVA type) with one part paint to three parts glue. Apply paint to large areas with a sponge, a cloth, or your fingers; use a brush for small areas. Clean brushes with acetone immediately after use.

On foam-rubber heads, spray paints are useful for large areas. Otherwise, spread emulsion and acrylic paints on to the surface of the foam with your fingertips. If the paints are applied with a brush, they tend to soak into the foam, which will remain wet and squelchy for a long time. If the head is covered in a fabric such as towelling, you might find artists' ink, applied with a very fine airbrush, helpful for colouring it.

Flesh hues can be mixed from varying quantities of white, yellow, red and brown. Ready-mixed flesh colours are seldom satisfactory, but they can provide a useful base with which to mix other colours.

Pure white eyeballs tend to look bare and staring, so mix a slightly creamy colour. Generally, the more the white of the eye is showing, the less friendly the character appears; large pupils suggest a warmer character. It can be very effective to paint the whole eyeball a dark colour, such as blue, black, purple or green.

Fig 61 Characters designed and carved in wood by John Wright for *Rapunzel* by the Little Angel Theatre. Rapunzel's hair is rayon crochet thread, the Prince's is fur, and the Witch's is ostrich feathers

Eyebrows can be painted or made from the same material as the hair. With very fair hair, the eyebrows tend to be a little darker.

Acrylic varnish may be used to enhance any parts that need emphasis, such as eyeballs, but you should generally avoid varnish for the same reasons why you avoid shiny paints. When wet, the varnish has a milky appearance, but it dries clear.

Hair

Hair is sometimes modelled with the head and painted but it is usually more effective to glue on suitable materials, either directly to the head or by creating a wig. A wide variety of materials may be used, such as knitting wool, rug wool, synthetic fur fabric, embroidery silks, feathers, rope or string (dyed if necessary), wood shavings, or strips of felt fabric. The only definitely unsuitable materials are real hair and real fur.

4 Construction Techniques

Before proceeding with any aspect of puppet construction, read carefully the advice in Chapter 2, as this will influence which construction techniques you adopt. The techniques offered here each identify for which type of puppet they are appropriate.

HEADS

Make heads by any of the methods described in Chapter 3. Choose materials and methods which are consistent with the type of puppet required and the jointing methods proposed.

Fig 62 Amahl's Mother, a rod puppet for Menotti's *Amahl and the Night Visitors* by the Little Angel Theatre. Designed by Lyndie Wright and carved in wood by John Wright

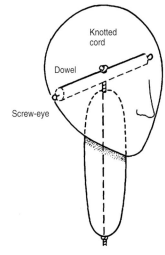

Fig 63 (a) A horizontal dowelling insert for securing the neck and the head strings;

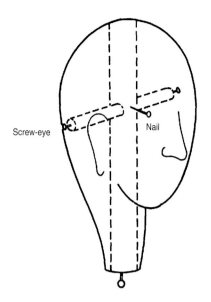

Screw-eye   Nail

Fig 63 (b) a dowelling 'cross' built into the head

For a marionette, make the ears strong enough for attaching head strings. If they are not strong enough, at an appropriate stage in construction *either* secure a strong dowel across the head for attaching screw-eyes, and for attaching the neck, *or*, if the head and neck are built in one piece, build a dowelling cross into the head. This is a large vertical dowel with a hole drilled through it to accommodate a horizontal dowel, which is glued in place. Use screw-eyes for attaching head strings, and another in the bottom of the neck for the joint with the body.

NECKS AND NECK JOINTS

Neck Built on to the Body

ROD PUPPETS OR MARIONETTES

Drill a hole across the neck and in either side of the head, near the ears. Drill holes through two short dowels to act as spacers to keep the neck in place. Insert a piece of thick wire through the holes in the head, the neck and the dowel spacers. Cut off the ends of the wire and secure it in the head with glue and more of the material used for the head, applied inside and outside the head. This method restricts head movement to nodding.

Alternatively, with a rubber head, do not cut the wire; bend the ends over into a loop and push each end back into the head near where it emerged. This loop also provides a fixture for marionette head strings.

MARIONETTES

To allow the head to nod and turn, instead of drilling a hole through the neck, fasten a screw-eye in the top of the neck and proceed as previously.

Neck Built on to the Head

MARIONETTES

To join the neck to the body, use screw-eyes joined by string, or a string through a hole in the body and a screw-eye in the neck. These methods presuppose a dowel built into the neck. Do not use interlocked screw-eyes, as they can catch in awkward positions.

ROD PUPPETS OPERATED FROM BEHIND

The neck may be created with a rounded base to fit into a hollow in the body. A strong cord from side to side through the neck passes though holes in the body and is secured by knotting the ends. This permits quite a range of movement (via a short control rod to the back of the neck), while preventing the head from turning too far.

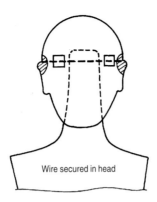

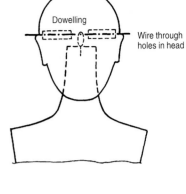

Fig 64 Different methods for fixing the neck joint – (a) wire through the neck, secured in the head, permits nodding but not turning;

Fig 64 (b) a wire through a screw-eye permits nodding and some turning;

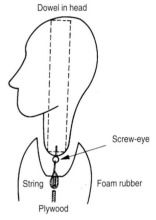

Fig 64 (c) two screw-eyes joined by string;

Fig 64 (d) a screw-eye and string;

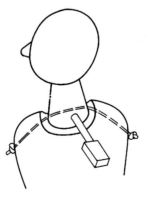

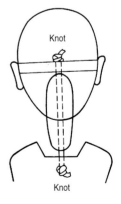

Fig 64 (e) a cord through neck and body;

Fig 64 (f) a neck separate from head and body, attached by cord (the recommended method for marionettes)

Neck Separate from Head and Body

MARIONETTES

Any of the joints described above may be used to join the neck to the head and body, but this method permits greater scope for movement, and smoother, more natural movement. The neck is usually carved from wood or shaped from a thick dowel.

To join the neck to the head, drill a hole through the mid-point of a dowel that is the internal width of the head. Thread a piece of knotted cord through the hole, then secure the dowel horizontally in the head, between the ears.

Drill a hole through the full length of the neck, thread the cord through this hole and secure the end to the body. To assist smooth movement, round the ends of the neck, or insert a wooden ball between the neck and the body.

EYES

Non-Moving Eyes

For all types of puppet, eyes can be carved, modelled or cast with the other features and then painted, or they can be suggested in many ways.

Glue into hollow eye sockets buttons, wooden balls or beads, appropriately painted and varnished, or cut a ball in half and use the two pieces. Hollow eye sockets can be painted a dark colour, and varnished if required, or covered with a reflective material such as metallic spangles. Deep slits can be made in the eye sockets to produce heavy shadow, or the shape of the eyeballs can be cut out and a small wooden bead (often black), glued top and bottom, placed in the centre of the hole.

Glass (medical or dolls') eyes can be used, but are too naturalistic for most puppets.

Fig 65 Venus designed and carved in wood by John Wright for the Little Angel Theatre's production of *Cupid and Psyche*

Moving Eyes

For rod puppets and marionettes, eye movement can be most expressive, but it is effective only for fairly intimate performances, as it will not show from a distance. It is built in at an early stage of the head-making process, and is best suited to a modelled head.

Make the eyes from two wooden balls (the size depends on the size of the head), with a hole drilled through the centre of each ball. Pivot the balls on a piece of strong galvanized wire (12- or 14-gauge), using 12mm diameter dowelling to give the necessary spacing between the eyes.

Build the balls and wire into the plasticine shape and cover with the appropriate separator (*see* page 35).

Fig 66 Moving eyes –
(a) wooden eyes built into
a plasticine base before
the head is modelled;

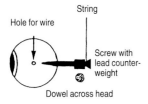

Fig 66 (b) the mechanism
for opening and closing the
eyes;

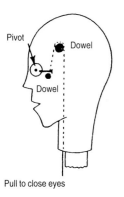

Fig 66 (c) moving eyes for
a rod puppet

Model the head over this shape, leaving the desired amount of eyeball uncovered and the ends of the wire projecting through each side of the head. When the head is cut open and the plasticine removed, remove and clean the balls, then fix a screw weighted with lead into the back of each ball; some makers use a spring instead of a weight. This acts as a counterbalance to open the eyes after they have been closed. They are closed by means of a string attached to the end of each screw.

Replace the balls in the head, cut the wire to the required length and secure it in the head by covering the ends with the same material as that used to model the head.

To stop the eyes opening too far, fix a thin dowel rod across the head for the screws to rest on. If the modelling material shrinks and the eyes jam in the head, this can usually be put right by running a sharp knife around the inside of the eyelids. Paint the eyes on the wooden balls when the face is painted.

For a marionette, the eye strings pass through two holes in the head. To prevent the thread fraying, it is a good idea to glue a piece of plastic drinking straw into the hole and wax the strings thoroughly with beeswax.

For a rod puppet, the strings pass over another dowel, fastened across the head, and then run down to a trigger mechanism on the control.

MOVING MOUTHS

Hand Puppets

A moving mouth may be made by cutting out two pieces of plywood for the jaws. Glue and tack a cloth hinge to the plywood. Tack strips of canvas or web-

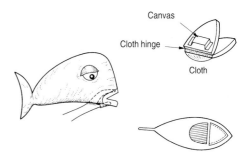

Fig 67 A moving mouth made from wood

Fig 68 The Devil from *Faustus* by Barry Smith's Theatre of Puppets. The head is modelled in paste and paper

bing to the plywood to contain your hand. Secure the plywood to the head with glue and a method appropriate to the material being used. Insert your fingers into the canvas strip in the upper jaw and your thumb into the lower jaw to hold the puppet and move the mouth.

Rod Puppets and Marionettes

While hand puppets may make a feature of a moving mouth, this facility is

Fig 69 A moving mouth in a modelled head: a puppet from the Harlequin Theatre, Colwyn Bay, and now in the Puppet Centre Collection

not often required for other types of puppet – and can be a liability. It must not move indiscriminately with no regard to speech, yet it would be impossible (and undesirable) to move it to every syllable. Its most effective use can be to give a gasp or similar reaction.

For a rod puppet or marionette, model the head over a plasticine base. When the head is cut open and the plasticine removed, carefully cut the mouth (the lower lip and chin in an L-shape) from the head. Glue a wooden block inside this L-shaped piece and strengthen the bond with the material used to make the head.

Drill a hole through the block and pivot it on a piece of galvanized wire (12- or 14-gauge). Drill holes in the sides of the head to accommodate the ends of the wire.

Attach a string to the back of the block for opening the mouth. The string passes through the top of the head for a marionette, and over a dowel secured in the head then down to a trigger mechanism for a rod puppet. The weight of the block acts as a counterbalance to close the mouth. A screw weighted with lead may be attached to the back of the block to increase the weight.

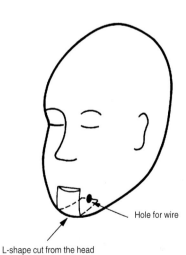

L-shape cut from the head

Hole for wire

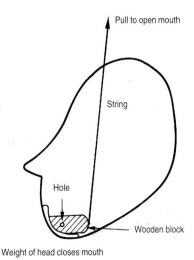

Pull to open mouth

String

Hole

Wooden block

Weight of head closes mouth

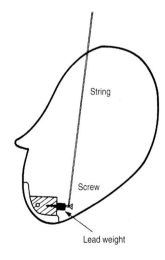

String

Screw

Lead weight

Fig 70 Making a moving mouth –
(a) the mouth shape cut from the head;

Fig 70 (b) the mechanism with a wooden block as a counterweight;

Fig 70 (c) the mechanism with a screw and lead as a counterweight

BODIES FOR GLOVE AND HAND PUPPETS

A Glove Puppet Body

It is recommended that the basic glove is made from curtain lining or a jersey material and the costume sewn or glued on to it. This makes it easier to achieve a good fit and prolongs the life of the costume.

First, make a paper pattern: fold a sheet of paper in half lengthways, lay one hand on the paper in the operating position and draw round the outline, but not too close to the hand. Allow a margin of about 2cm (¾in) around your hand and 3cm (1¼in) on each side of your arm. If the puppet will always be used on this hand, proceed to the next stage below; if it might be used on either hand, turn your hand over and replace it on the pattern. Draw around your hand in this position, then make a smooth curve around both outlines.

Ensure that the neck is wide enough to go over the puppet's neck after it is stitched, that the body is wide enough to get your hand in and out easily, and that the glove is long enough to reach almost to your elbow. Then cut out the paper pattern.

Lay the pattern on to a double thickness of material, right side to right side, and mark out the body shape. If you need a very wide neck, pin a tuck in the fabric before marking out the pattern (remove the pins to open the tuck after the glove is stitched). Stitch around the outline, leaving the neck and the bottom open.

Try the glove for comfort on both hands; if necessary, unpick and restitch. Cut out the glove within 5–6mm (¼in) of the stitching and snip into the corners between neck and arms. Cut right up to (but not through) the stitch-

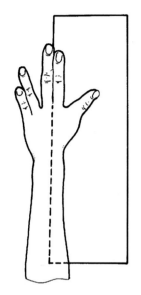

Fig 71 (a) Making a paper pattern for a glove body;

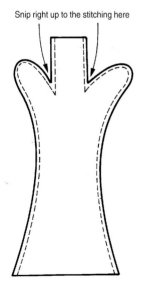

Snip right up to the stitching here

Fig 71 (b) the body shape;

Fig 71 (c) a loop and hook bent from a piece of wire;

Fig 71 (d) the loop of wire fixed in the hem of the glove body;

ing, or the glove will pull at these points when reversed. Reverse the glove so that the seams are inside.

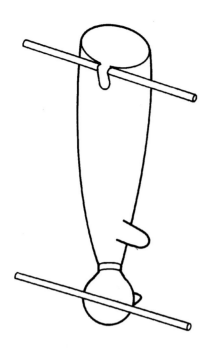

Fig 71 (e) the puppet hanging in the booth ready for use

Glue the glove to the puppet's neck, securing it with a strong draw-thread.

Bend a length of 12- or 14-gauge galvanized wire into a loop with a portion of it forming a hook. Stitch or glue the loop into the hem at the bottom of the glove. The hook enables you to hang up the puppet in the booth and the loop holds the bottom open for speedy insertion of your hand during a show.

Finally, fit the costume on to the glove.

Animal Bodies for Glove Puppets

You may combine the traditional glove puppet body with an animal head. Alternatively, create the normal glove, but add a body of foam rubber covered with fabric, or a fabric body stuffed with wadding. The operating hand is bent at the wrist, so that the body sits horizontally on the back of the hand and arm. Insert your fingers into the head and front limbs as with other glove puppets. Stuff the hind legs with wadding or foam rubber.

Animal Bodies for Hand Puppets

The following methods are useful when a firm body structure is required for a hand puppet rather than a simple fabric sleeve.

◆ Sculpt the shape in foam rubber. This will often require a separate jaw, hinged to the main body with a fabric or canvas hinge glued on. Cut away the body and jaw to accommodate your hand.

◆ Create a basic structure with chicken wire (wire mesh). Cover it with a light modelling material, or card and glue, or sheet foam rubber and fabric. It will need something for you to hold it by, such as a dowel rod fixed securely across the body.

◆ Build up the required shape in strong card (*see* page 35). Build a dowelling handle into the structure. Cover the shape with a modelling material or any suitable fabric.

◆ Cast the body in latex rubber as for a head (*see* page 38).

Mouth Puppet Bodies

Mouth puppets (*see* page 17) may have simply a head and wide costume 'sleeve' for the body, but this costume

Fig 72 An animal body built on to the basic glove

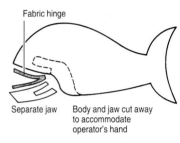

Fig 73 (a) A foam-rubber animal body;

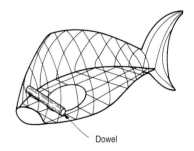

Fig 73 (b) a frame of chicken wire as the base for a body

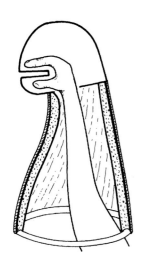

Fig 74 A 'mouth puppet' head and a fabric body lined with foam rubber to maintain the required bulk

might need some bulk for characterization. If so, line the costume with sheet foam rubber of suitable thickness, to achieve not only the bulk but also the flexibility required.

ROD PUPPET SHOULDER BLOCKS

The shoulder block may be shaped from wood or plywood padded with foam rubber. Drill a hole through the block to accommodate the central rod; make sure it moves freely if the head is to turn. It may be secured to the central rod with a supporting collar or suspended on cord.

A Supporting Collar

This allows 360-degree turning of the head. The best method is to drill a hole, the same diameter as the central rod, through a block of wood 20mm (¾in) thick. Then, with a suitable saw or chisel, cut it into a circle with a diameter about 3cm (1¼in) greater than

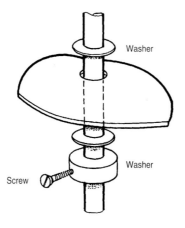

Fig 75 (a) A wooden supporting collar for a plywood and foam-rubber shoulder block;

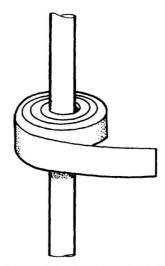

Fig 75 (b) card glued and bound tightly around the central rod to form a supporting collar;

the hole. Drill before shaping to reduce the risk of the collar splitting. Finally, screw it to the rod.

Alternatively, cut a long strip of card, then glue, wind and bind it tightly around the central rod to create the supporting collar.

To ensure that the shoulders do not grip on this supporting collar, make a 'washer' to insert between the two; the lids and bases of smooth plastic containers are ideal. If the head and neck are built in one piece, you will need another washer between the bottom of the neck and any foam-rubber shoulder padding; ensure that the neck cannot touch any part of the foam rubber.

Cord Fastening

Cord may be used to suspend the shoulder block on the central rod. This permits some natural movement of the body and some degree of turning for the head.

Drill two holes through the shoulder block, one on either side of the hole for

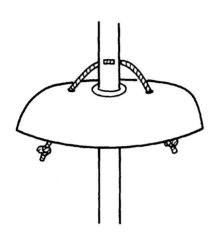

Fig 75 (c) a shoulder block suspended on a cord through the central rod

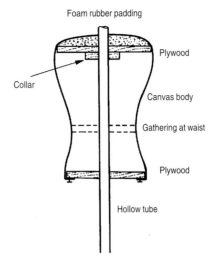

Foam rubber padding

Plywood

Collar

Canvas body

Gathering at waist

Plywood

Hollow tube

Fig 76 A plywood and canvas body

the central rod. Drill another hole across the central rod, just above the position for the top of the shoulder block. Thread a piece of cord though this hole and down through the two holes in the shoulder block and knot the ends at a suitable length. Seal the knots with glue.

A Rod Puppet Body on a Shoulder Block

You can attach to the shoulder block a suitable material that will give more substance to the body, for example, sheet foam rubber, cardboard or buckram.

Alternatively, a body may be made from a tube of canvas, or some other strong material, glued and tacked to the shoulder block at the top and to a piece of plywood at the bottom. Clearly, this lower piece must have a hole in the centre to accommodate the main rod. Gather in the waist with draw-threads.

BODIES FOR ROD PUPPETS AND MARIONETTES

A rod puppet might have a body rather than a just a shoulder block. This may be just a thorax, a whole body in one piece, or a separate thorax and pelvis, for puppets that need to bend at the waist and have attachments for legs. The body is attached to the central rod with a supporting collar, in the same way as a shoulder block.

For a marionette, a jointed thorax and pelvis provide the best movement and a neck separate from head and body is normally the best design.

A Modelled Body

Model the body following the techniques described in Chapter 3. For extra strength, it may be made on a basic shape of balsa wood or polystyrene, which then remains inside the body.

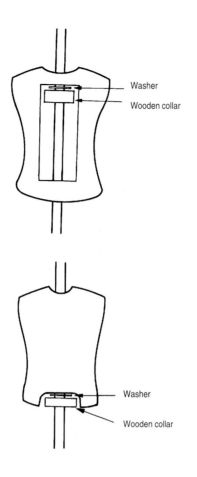

Fig 77 (a) Supporting collars for hollow and solid rod-puppet bodies;

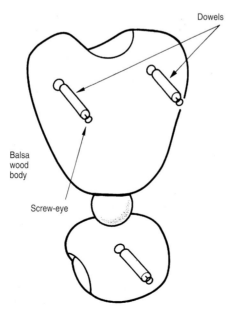

Fig 77 (b) making secure fixtures for strings in a balsa-wood body for a marionette

Washer
Wooden collar

Washer
Wooden collar

Dowels
Balsa wood body
Screw-eye

A Carved Body

Before carving, design the whole puppet and determine the waist joint. The usual techniques for wood-carving (*see* Chapter 3) may be employed, or balsa wood may be shaped with rasps and glasspaper. Do not use balsa wood if the whole puppet is carved.

A wooden thorax might need hollowing out to reduce its weight. Work from underneath, cutting up into the thorax. With thorax and pelvis carved in one piece, cut it open lengthways, hollow it, then re-join the two parts with wood-working adhesive. If a supporting collar is required for a rod puppet, attach this at an appropriate stage of construction.

If balsa wood is used for a marionette body, secure fixtures are needed for attaching strings. Glue short dowels into holes drilled in the body and fix small screw-eyes in the dowels. Angle the drill upwards so that the dowels cannot be pulled out by tension on the control strings.

A Cast Body

Model the body (in one or two pieces) in plasticine on dowels and take a plaster cast, as described in Chapter 3. When the dowels in the body are removed from the casts, they will leave holes in the plaster through which latex rubber can be poured; this will also leave holes in the body parts that can be used later for joining them.

Cast the body in a suitable material. If rubber is used, allow it to form a fairly thick layer or it will not hold its shape when the puppet is assembled.

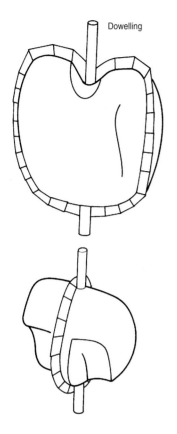

Dowelling

Fig 78 Dividing the plasticine models for casting a body in plaster

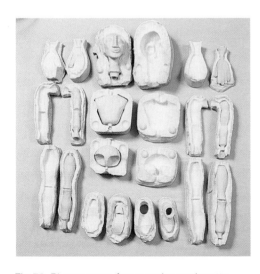

Fig 79 Plaster casts for an entire marionette opened to reveal the latex parts inside

A Wood and Foam-Rubber Body

This method is suitable only for marionettes. Make the thorax by gluing foam rubber to a piece of plywood, or hardboard, cut to the shape required. With scissors, snip the foam rubber into the required three-dimensional form.

To make the pelvis, saw two sections from a block of wood, leaving a T-shape. Round off the sharp corners and pad the block with foam rubber. Alternatively, glue and screw together two pieces of wood in the T-shape and pad to shape.

Animal Bodies

Any of the methods described above for modelled, sculpted or cast bodies may be used for animal rod puppets or marionettes. For strength, durability and lightness, it is a good idea to build modelled bodies on a basic frame of cardboard, polystyrene or balsa wood. Before beginning any construction, you need to be aware of the following important considerations.

Modelled or carved wooden bodies may be appropriate for painting without further covering. Other types of body are usually covered with a material that might need to be dyed to the required colour, or painted with suitable markings using diluted acrylic paints.

A rod puppet central control may be glued securely into a solid body; for security, insert a piece of 12- or 14-gauge galvanized wire through the body and through a small hole drilled across the rod. This can be fiddly but worthwhile: careful measuring helps. Alternatively, screw or build into the body a block of wood, with a hole

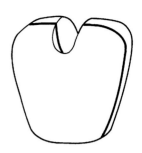

Fig 80 Making a marionette from wood and foam rubber – (a) foam rubber glued to a plywood body shape;

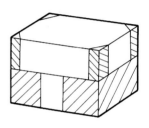

Fig 80 (b) the shaded parts are cut from the block to form the pelvis;

Foam rubber padding

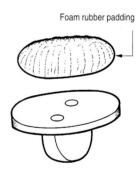

Fig 80 (c) two pieces of shaped wood joined and padded with foam rubber for the pelvis

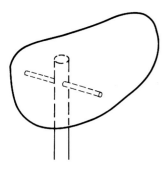

Fig 81 (a) Securing a rod-puppet control with a piece of stiff wire;

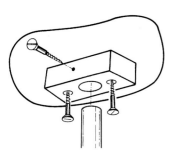

Fig 81 (b) a central rod that fits into a block built into the body;

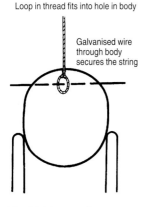

Loop in thread fits into hole in body

Galvanised wire through body secures the string

Fig 81 (c) securing a marionette string to a body that is unsuitable for a screw-eye

drilled in it of the same diameter as the control rod. Secure the control rod in the hole with glue, or a screw through the side of the block; this is helpful for a removable rod for packing.

Attach marionette body strings direct to holes in a strong centre piece of the body; if this is not possible, you might need a little ingenuity – for example, tie the thread to a button inside a hollow body, or push a length of galvanized wire through a polystyrene or balsa-wood body, and through a loop in the end of the thread.

A CARDBOARD BODY

Make a cardboard body in the same way as a cardboard head. Cut a basic profile shape from strong card or, preferably, a thin sheet of plywood. Make a hole in the neck for a cord for the neck joint. Make two holes in the card to accommodate 18mm (¾in)

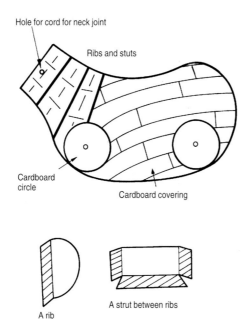

Hole for cord for neck joint

Ribs and stuts

Cardboard circle

Cardboard covering

A rib

A strut between ribs

Fig 82 A cardboard body for an animal

diameter dowels (for attaching the legs later), and glue the dowels into the holes. Glue 'ribs' and strengthening pieces to the basic shape, then cover it with card. Over the end of each dowel, glue a circle of smooth card on which the legs may turn.

Cover the cardboard body with a modelling material, nylon 'hair', synthetic fur fabric, knitting wool fluffed up, cloth, or any other suitable material. Cover the neck joint with material and then finish it in the same way as the body.

A SCULPTED BODY

When a rod puppet animal has no legs, or legs that simply dangle from the body, you may shape the body from foam rubber, polystyrene or balsa wood and cover it as appropriate (*see* Chapter 3).

A SCULPTED BODY WITH WORKING LEGS

Cut out a plywood profile body shape with a coping saw or band-saw. Drill a hole in the neck for a cord. Glue blocks

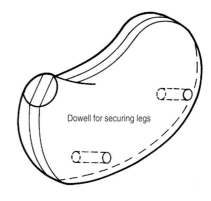

Dowell for securing legs

Fig 83 A plywood body shape padded with foam rubber and with dowel inserts for attaching the legs

of foam rubber, polystyrene or balsa wood to each side of the plywood and shape it appropriately. Drill two holes for dowels for attaching the legs, *see* the instructions opposite for a cardboard body. Glue and insert the dowels and cover the ends with smooth card. Then cover the body with material, such as wool, fur fabric, and so on.

A FLEXIBLE BODY

This is particularly suitable for rod puppets. The construction is based on a central core of rope, flexible tubing, curtain wire, or a spring of light steel

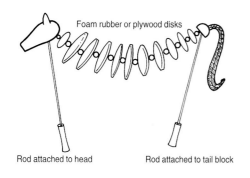

Foam rubber or plywood disks

Rod attached to head   Rod attached to tail block

Fig 84 (a) A flexible body constructed on a core of rope or tubing;

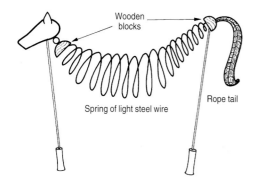

Wooden blocks

Spring of light steel wire   Rope tail

Fig 84 (b) a body made of a coiled spring

wire, secured directly to the head and tail, or attached at each end to a block of wood.

The body parts are threaded on the core rope or tubing; for example, they could be discs of foam rubber, graduated in diameter, with smaller pieces as spacers, or blocks of polystyrene shaped to permit flexing of the body. This may simply be painted but is usually covered with fabric or some other appropriate material.

A coiled spring may be covered with fabric trimming wound around the wire, or it may be completely covered in fabric.

WAIST JOINTS

These joints are used most frequently for marionettes, but may also be used for rod puppets operated from behind rather than from below, with a short main control rod attached either to the head and held inside the thorax (*see* Fig 27), or to the back of the neck (*see* Fig 64(e)).

LEATHER JOINTS

Real or synthetic leather joints may be used on bodies modelled on a solid base, on solid, sculpted bodies, and on those made from plywood padded with another material.

Cut slots in each section. Glue the ends of the strip of leather and insert them in the slots. Secure the leather further with nails.

If you want a restricted joint, permitting movement in only one direction, make the joint so that the thorax and pelvis are in contact. Cut away part of the thorax and pelvis to facilitate movement in the direction required.

Alternatively, use a strip of leather (or canvas) cut to the shape of the

Fig 85 Waist joints –
(a) a leather joint that
permits bending but not
turning;

Fig 85 (b) a restricted joint
that allows only forward
movement;

Fig 85 (c) a central strip of
leather can be used for
both waist and hip joints;

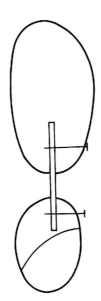
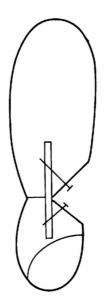
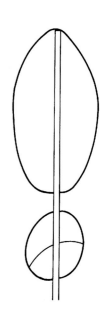

entire body, with sufficient extra length to make hip joints if required. Glue the front and back of the body to this, with enough space between thorax and pelvis to permit bending.

BALL JOINTS

These joints allow excellent movement. The second type is used frequently for unclothed bodies, but is recommended for most purposes.

For plywood and foam-rubber bodies, drill a hole in the plywood base of the thorax, and through a wooden ball; insert a screw-eye in the top of the pelvis. Join the pelvis and thorax with cord, with the ball between the two to facilitate smooth movement.

For carved and modelled bodies, make the body with hollows or holes in the pelvis and thorax, partially to accommodate a suitably large wooden ball. Drill two parallel holes through the ball and through the thorax and pelvis. On each side of the body thread a cord through all three sections, and knot the ends where they emerge from the body. Sink the knots in the body

and seal them with glue. Where necessary, cover the knots with a modelling material.

Alternatively, construct the body parts so that the bottom of the thorax and top of the pelvis are rounded, not hollowed. Join them with a single cord threaded through a wooden ball as a spacer for the waist.

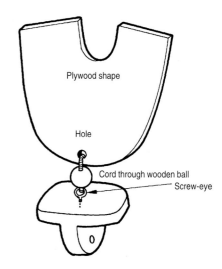

Fig 85 (d) a cord joint with a wooden ball used to improve movement;

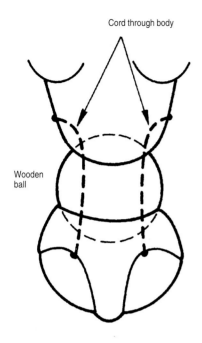

Fig 85 (e) a very flexible ball joint;

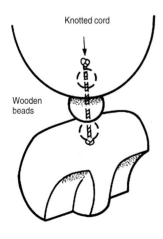

Fig 85 (f) a ball joint suitable for rubber bodies

This method is particularly suitable for use with rubber puppets as the body is able to roll on the ball without clinging to it. To secure the cord in rubber bodies, thread a bead on the cord on each side of the wooden ball; knot and glue the ends. Glue one bead into the thorax and the other into the pelvis.

ARMS, ELBOWS AND SHOULDER JOINTS

Arms

ROPE ARMS

Strong rope, knotted inside – or built into – the body, is used most often for rod puppets, whose arms go where you put them, rather than marionettes. It is sometimes used as a design feature when the rope is going to show. It provides some firmness, but also allows total flexibility of movement.

FOAM-RUBBER ARMS

Foam rubber may be trimmed to shape and threaded and glued on to a rope. Make a loop in the end of a piece of coat-hanger wire and use this like a needle to thread the rope through the arms; alternatively, slit the arms open lengthways with a craft knife, position the rope, and close the slot with glue.

LATEX-RUBBER ARMS

Arms may be cast in rubber, as for a head; for an idea of where to divide the plasticine model for creating the plaster cast, *see* Fig 86(a). To permit bending, when the arm is dry cut through the strip of rubber at the back of the elbow joint, leaving the front intact.

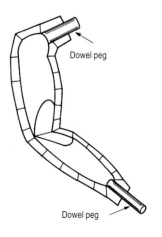

Fig 86 Arms and elbow joints – (a) plasticine arm ready for casting;

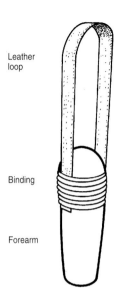

Leather loop

Binding

Forearm

Fig 86 (b) a wood and leather arm;

CARVED OR DOWELLING ARMS

Arms may be carved from wood or made from two pieces of dowelling built up with a suitable modelling material, or shaped down as necessary. Do not use thin dowel with no bulk for the arms.

If you want a less restricted elbow, there is an alternative to a conventional elbow joint (*see* Elbow Joints, below). You can use a long strip of leather for the upper arm, especially on a rod puppet. The ends of the leather strip are glued and either tacked or bound with thread to the top of the forearm. This leather loop replaces the upper arm and facilitates attachment to the body.

Elbow Joints

OPEN MORTISE AND TENON JOINTS

Join wooden arms at the elbow by cutting a deep groove in the upper arm to accommodate a tongue created by cutting away part of the forearm. Take care to leave enough wood on each section at the back of the elbow to prevent it bending in the wrong direction. The tongue fits in the groove and pivots on a nail through the upper arm. Ensure that the hole in the tongue and the size of the groove are sufficient to permit clean movement without any loose wobbling.

For smaller puppets, a wooden elbow joint may be too fragile. One alternative is to cut the tongue from a piece of sheet aluminium, using tin-snips and a file, and to glue and pin this in a slot cut in the lower arm.

LEATHER JOINTS

A leather joint has considerable flexibility, but maintains good control. It is

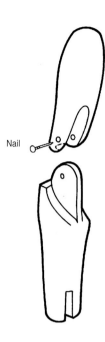

Nail

Fig 86 (c) an open mortise and tenon elbow joint;

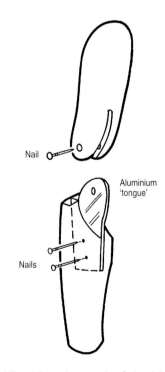

Nail

Aluminium 'tongue'

Nails

Fig 86 (d) a joint using a strip of aluminium;

also a neat method for a bare arm. Cut slots in each half of the arm at the elbow, and cut away wedges from the front of the elbow to permit bending. Glue and insert the leather in the slot and secure with nails. It helps to use a wider piece of leather so that you can pull it into the slot, then trim it to the arm width when secure.

Alternatively, cut a fine slot in the top of the forearm; to do this, drill a series of tiny holes and clean out the waste with a sharp craft knife. Glue a small loop of leather into the slot: it is fiddly to get it in – ease it in with a small tool such as a chisel – but it must be a good fit, and not loose. Secure it with tiny nails. Make a small, square-cornered staple from galvanized wire, put it through the leather loop, and glue the staple into small holes drilled in the upper arm. The whole joint must

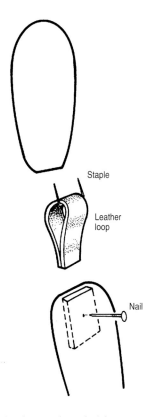

Fig 86 (f) a leather and staple joint

be sufficiently close for the arm parts to meet and prevent a double-jointed elbow, but not so tight as to restrict movement.

Shoulder Joints

CORD JOINTS

Strong cord through a hole or screw-eye in the top of the arm and tied to the body makes a satisfactory shoulder joint. If you are using body materials that are unsuitable for attaching the cord, such as polystyrene, foam rubber or balsa wood, you will need to insert a piece of galvanized wire across the body; loop the ends to provide fixings for the cord.

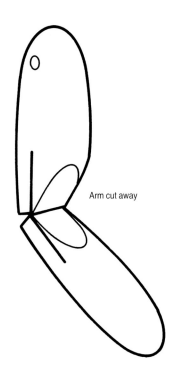

Fig 86 (e) a leather elbow joint;

LEATHER JOINTS

The leather loop and staple joint is excellent for wooden arms and body; ensure the leather loop is sufficiently loose to permit a full range of arm movement.

A JOINT FOR RUBBER PUPPETS

To effect the shoulder joint for a latex rubber puppet, use two wooden beads joined by strong cord knotted at each end. Glue one bead into the top of the arm and the other into the body.

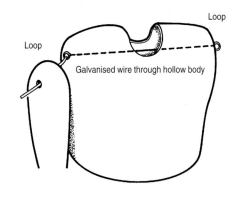

Fig 87 (c) a cord and wire joint for a solid body in lightweight materials;

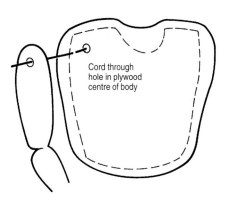

Fig 87 Shoulder joints – (a) a cord joint for a hollow body;

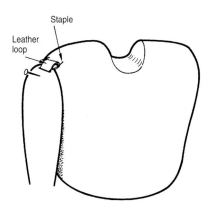

Fig 87 (d) a leather loop and staple joint;

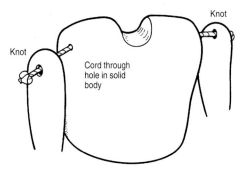

Fig 87 (b) a cord shoulder joint for a solid body;

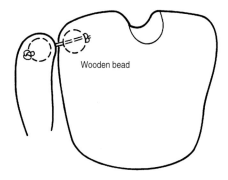

Fig 87 (e) a cord and beads joint for latex-rubber puppets

HANDS AND WRIST JOINTS

Hands

The shape of the hands is important in helping to create character, and characterless hands may spoil an otherwise exciting puppet. Hands can be simply shaped – detailed modelling is quite unnecessary – or indeed stylized (it is not uncommon for puppets to have only three fingers and a thumb), but the fingers should be held in an expressive manner.

When making hands, have regard for the wrist joint you intend to use. Some methods of jointing can be built in, rather than being added later. Hands for glove puppets may be made with a hollow wrist or cuff to accommodate your fingers for manipulation (*see* Fig 14(b)).

CLOTH HANDS

First, cut out two shapes, either mitten-shaped or with fingers. Stitch the two shapes together inside out, and then reverse. Where appropriate, stuff the fingers with foam rubber or wadding. This technique is most often used for glove puppets (*see* Fig 103), but occasionally a cloth hand with floppy fingers may be used for a rod puppet or marionette (*see* Fig 198), usually for comical characters.

CARVED WOODEN HANDS

Hands may be carved from wood, following the basic principles for carving a head. Begin by marking out the hand shape and leave spare wood at the wrist for securing in a vice; this can also be used, hollowed, for a wrist for glove puppets. Make saw cuts between the fingers, then carefully pare away at the fingers individually and hollow out the palm of the hand.

Remember that hands held naturally are not flat and stiff, nor are the fingers all held in the same plane. The thumb is also set in a different plane from the fingers.

FOAM-RUBBER HANDS

Cut the hands with sharp scissors following the same principles of shaping as for wood-carving. This type of hand is not really suitable for a marionette. Use foam rubber for the hands only when the head is made of foam rubber.

MODELLED HANDS

Milliput, an epoxy putty, may be used for modelling hands. For the general principles of working with it, *see* Chapter 3. To make hands, first intertwine pipe cleaners and bend them into the required position. Mix the putty; when mixed it has quite adhesive properties, so it can be pressed straight on to the pipe-cleaner hand. Use pieces of a reasonable size; you do not need to attach it to the fingers individually. Snip between the fingers with a pair of scissors and then model the shape of the fingers. The use of water facilitates the modelling and smoothing of the hands. In a short time, when it is set and cured, build up, cut away and smooth the hands as necessary.

When hands are intended for a glove puppet, glue a strong cardboard 'cuff' to each hand (*see* Fig 14(b)), and cover the card with the epoxy putty too.

LATEX-RUBBER HANDS

Rubber hands are cast in the same way as a rubber head. Fig 88(d) shows alternative ways to place the metal strips in the plasticine model to make the plas-

Fig 88 (a) The first stage in the construction of a wooden hand;

Fig 88 (b) the fingers are shaped and the palm hollowed out;

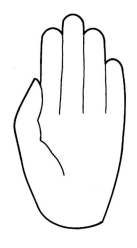

Fig 88 (c) the thumb is in a different plane from the fingers;

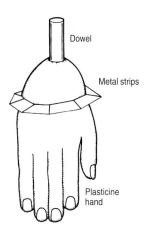

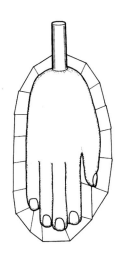

Fig 88 (d) two methods for placing the dividing metal strips when preparing a cast for a rubber hand

ter cast. When making hands for a glove puppet, model and cast the wrist and hand in one piece. When the latex-rubber hand is finished, you can stiffen the wrist with card if necessary.

Wrist Joints

Occasionally, hands for rod puppets are built on to the arms without any flexible wrist joint. In this case, the fingers must be in an interesting position in order to compensate for the lack of wrist movement. The control rod for such a hand is usually attached at the wrist.

The following joints are suitable for the wrists of rod puppets and marionettes. The method you choose depends on the degree of movement required and the materials used for hand and arm.

SEWN JOINTS

Fabric hands are stitched on to fabric glove puppets. In the unusual circumstance where fabric hands are attached to solid arms, they must be made with a wrist, so that this can be glued and bound to the forearm.

ROPE JOINTS

Glue the end of a rope arm directly into a hole in the heel of the hand, or into a slot cut along the palm.

LEATHER JOINTS

Glue and nail a strip of leather into a slot cut in the arm and hand; this restricts movement somewhat, which is desirable for some applications.

An alternative and more flexible leather joint, popular for carved puppets, is made by gluing and pinning the

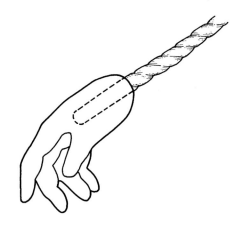

Fig 89 Wrist joints – (a) a rope glued into the hand;

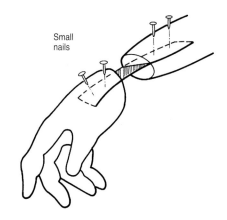

Fig 89 (b) a leather strap wrist joint;

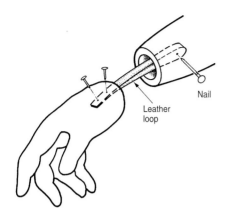

Fig 89 (c) a leather loop wrist joint;

Alternatively, attach the screw-eye to the hand and drill a fairly large hole upwards into the forearm; insert the screw-eye into the hole and secure it with a nail.

If the hand is made of latex rubber, glue a dowel inside it for attaching the screw-eye. If it is made of foam rubber, make a hole into the hand from the wrist to accommodate the dowel, which is glued securely in place. The dowel provides a strong fixture not only for the wrist joint, but also for attaching a control wire for a rod puppet, or a control string for a marionette.

ends of a 6mm (¼in) wide loop of leather into a slot cut in the hand. The loop fits into a hole drilled into the forearm and is secured with a nail.

SCREW-EYE JOINTS

Although it is generally not recommended, there are times when a screw-eye joint might be appropriate. A screw-eye in the hand may be attached to the forearm by cord through a small hole drilled in the arm.

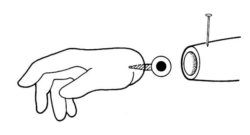

Fig 89 (e) a screw-eye pivots in a hole in the arm;

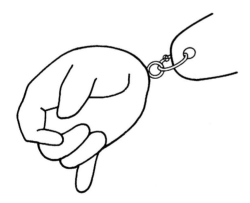

Fig 89 (d) a screw-eye and string wrist joint;

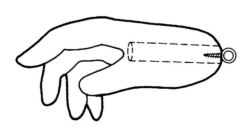

Fig 89 (f) a dowel in a foam rubber or latex hand provides a secure attachment for the wrist joint and a control string or rod;

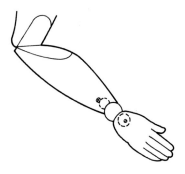

Fig 89 (g) a wrist joint for latex-rubber arms and hands

CORD AND BEAD JOINTS

Join latex-rubber hands to arms by gluing into them wooden beads joined by knotted cord. A bead *between* hand and arm promotes flowing movement but you need to plan for this when making the arms, or the hands will hang too low.

LEGS AND KNEE JOINTS

You must decide on the kind of ankle joint you plan to use before you make the legs.

Glove Puppet Legs

Use one of the techniques detailed below for constructing the lower leg and foot. Make the upper leg from a tube of strong material, such as calico or soft canvas, stuffed with wadding or foam rubber. Glue the tube to the lower leg and bind it with strong thread; stitch it to the glove puppet body. Such legs usually swing freely, controlled by the movement of the body.

If you wish to control them with the fingers of your free hand, the thighs must contain strong, hollow tubes. Alternatively, use a jointed wooden leg with the thigh hollowed out.

Make holes in the back of the upper thighs and oversew the material around the hole to prevent fraying. Insert the first two fingers of your free hand to operate the legs, using a glove and sleeve to disguise your hand and arm.

Carved and Dowelling Legs

Legs may be carved in wood or made from dowelling, either built up with a modelling material or shaped down.

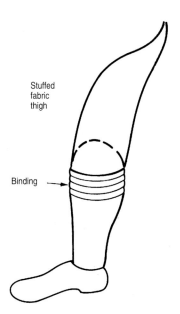

Fig 90 (a) A leg for a glove puppet;

Stuffed fabric thigh

Binding

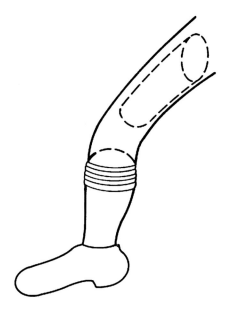

Fig 90 (b) a glove puppet leg for directly controlled movement

Two joints are suitable – an open mortise and tenon joint and a leather joint.

OPEN MORTISE AND TENON JOINT

Cut a groove in one part of the leg and a tongue in the other, shaping them to allow the leg to bend one way. Leave a ridge on the front of the knee to prevent it bending in the wrong direction.

Put the leg together and drill a hole across the joint. Enlarge the hole in the 'tongue' to allow it to pivot freely on the nail that is to secure the joint. Reassemble the leg, insert the nail, and secure it with glue.

LEATHER JOINT

Cut a slot in each leg section at the knee, then cut or file away a wedge shape behind the knee to permit bending. Glue a piece of leather into each slot and secure with small nails; the

leather must be short enough to allow the leg pieces to touch, and should fit tightly into the slots. It is a good idea to leave a little spare on the sides of the leather to enable you to pull it securely into the slots. Cut off the waste when the joint is completed.

Plywood Legs

Plywood shapes may be glued together in layers and the shaping refined with a rasp or a modelling material. Such legs are particularly suitable for animals but, depending on their size, can be rather heavy. An alternative, combining a central core of plywood, padded to shape with foam rubber, provides a very satisfactory leg and knee joint without too much weight. This would be suitable whenever the leg is to be costumed or, for an animal, if covered directly with fabric.

PLYWOOD AND FOAM-RUBBER LEG

This lighter version is made from four plywood shapes which form an open mortise and tenon knee joint. With a coping saw or band-saw, cut out four leg shapes 'A', *see* Fig 93(a). Make the lower leg from *slightly* thinner plywood and leave enough on the bottom of it to slot into the foot for the ankle joint.

Glue together the three thigh sections, forming a groove to accommodate the 'tongue' on the lower leg. Insert the tongue into the groove and drill through the joint at the point indicated. Enlarge the hole in the tongue and ensure the leg moves freely. Rejoin the leg with a nail and secure the head of the nail with glue.

Glue foam rubber on to the plywood and trim to shape. Ensure that the foam rubber does not cover the parts of the

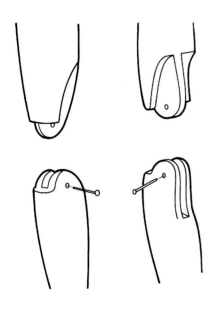

Fig 91 An open mortise and tenon joint for wooden legs

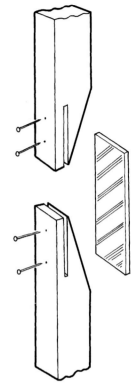

Fig 92 A leather knee joint – (a) the slot cut for the leather, and the rear corners cut away;

Fig 92 (b) securing the leather

Fig 93 (a) plywood leg
shapes;

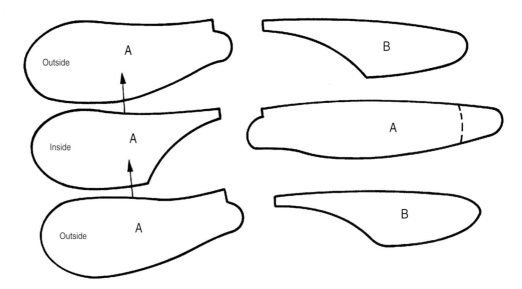

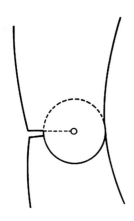

Fig 93 (b) the position of
the hole for jointing;

Fig 93 (c) the parts
assembled;

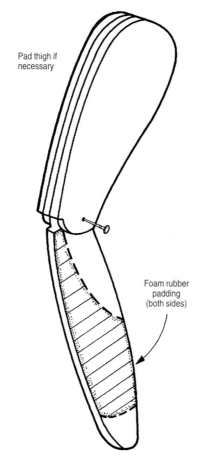

Pad thigh if
necessary

Foam rubber
padding
(both sides)

lower leg that fit into the groove in the
thigh or into the foot.

A LEG ENTIRELY IN PLYWOOD

For a leg entirely in plywood, cut out
six shapes 'A' and 'B' (*see* Fig 93(a)).
Use thicker plywood than for the plywood and foam-rubber leg, in order to
give the leg its bulk. Glue the shapes
together to create a mortise and tenon
joint. (Fig 93(d) shows a variation for
an animal leg.) When dry, refine by
shaping down or by building upon the
basic shape with foam rubber or a suitable modelling material such as Milliput (epoxy putty).

Latex-Rubber Legs

Rubber legs are moulded in one piece.
The procedure is the same as for a rubber head. Fig 94 shows the shape for
the plasticine model and how to place
the metal strips for making the plaster
cast. When the leg is made and the rubber is dry, make a slit across the front of
the knee joint, to allow it to bend.

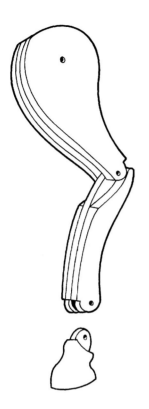

Fig 93 (d) plywood legs for an animal;

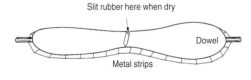

Slit rubber here when dry

Dowel

Metal strips

Fig 94 Placing the metal strips in a plasticine model for a plaster cast

HIP JOINTS

For sculpted legs, all of the following hip joints are possible; for other legs, the leather method is not suitable. Your selection will depend also on what material is used for the pelvis, and on whether you are making a rod puppet with a long central control rod.

GALVANIZED WIRE JOINT

Suspend the legs from a piece of 12-14 gauge galvanized wire. Insert it through holes drilled across the top of each thigh and the leg-divider. With pliers, bend each end of the wire upwards at a sharp right-angle, and bend the tips inwards so that they fit into holes drilled in the sides of the pelvis. Secure the wire with glue, and staples if necessary. This is the recommended method.

Alternatively, loop a strip of leather and glue and nail the ends in a slot in the top of the leg. Suspend the loop from a piece of galvanized wire.

Usually, rod puppet legs dangle freely but occasionally they are controlled by strings from below. If so, suspend them from a length of galvanized wire. Allow a fair length of leg above the wire to give good leverage for moving the legs.

CORD JOINT

Strong cord may be threaded through holes drilled across the tops of the legs, and through holes drilled up through the pelvis. Knot and glue the ends on top of the pelvis.

LEATHER JOINT

Real or synthetic leather is particularly useful. Glue one end of a leather strip into a slot in the top of the thigh; secure it with small nails if necessary. Secure the other end in the pelvis in the same manner.

Alternatively, the leather may run through the entire length of the body

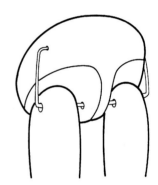

Fig 95 Hip joints –
(a) a wire joint;

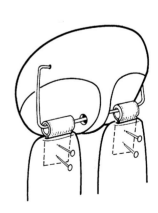

Fig 95 (b) a wire and
leather hip joint;

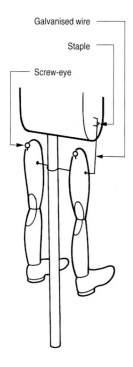

Galvanised wire

Staple

Screw-eye

Fig 95 (c) a hip joint for rod
puppet legs to be
controlled by strings;

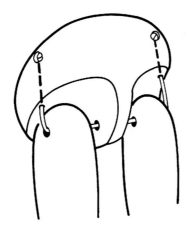

Fig 95 (d) a cord hip joint for a marionette;

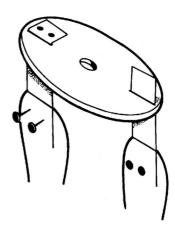

Fig 95 (g) a leather or canvas hip joint; the
leather thong is inserted in the slot, glued and
tacked down;

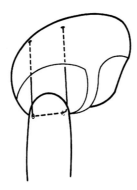

Fig 95 (e) a cord joint for a marionette or rod
puppet with a long central rod;

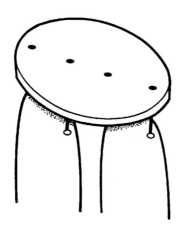

Fig 95 (f) a cord joint for a
wooden base to a body;

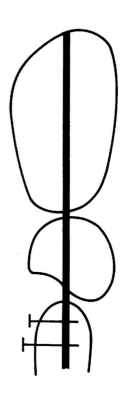

Fig 95 (h) a hip joint with a central leather strip
through the entire body

with enough remaining below the pelvis to effect the joint with the thigh.

Joints for Animals

SCREW JOINTS

Depending on the structure and composition of the body, animal legs may be attached to the body, or to dowels in the body, by screws with washers.

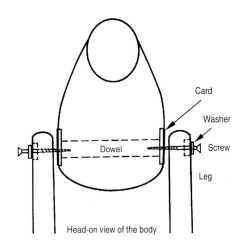

Fig 96 Joints for animals – (a) attaching legs to an animal body by means of screws;

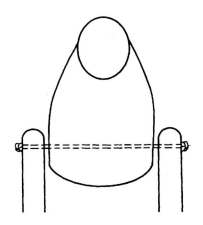

Fig 96 (b) a cord joint;

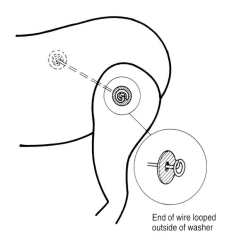

Fig 96 (c) a wire joint

CORD JOINTS

Legs may be joined by strong cord through the body; knot the cord on the outside of each leg. However, with some legs and body shapes there may be a tendency for the legs to swing inwards under the body, so use this method selectively.

WIRE JOINTS

The legs may be suspended on galvanized wire through the body with the ends looped outside of washers.

FEET AND ANKLE JOINTS

Carved and Modelled Feet

Carve or model feet using the techniques described in Chapter 3. To remove plasticine from a modelled foot, cut off the sole, then replace it when the foot is hollow. You can glue pieces of felt on to the soles of a marionette's feet, to prevent them making too much noise on the stage floor.

Open Mortise and Tenon Ankle Joint

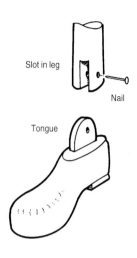

Slot in leg

Nail

Tongue

Fig 97 (a) An ankle joint with the slot in the leg;

To make an effective ankle joint, *either* build a tongue on to the foot to fit into a slot in the leg, *or* make a slot in the foot (by drilling a series of holes and clearing the waste with a chisel or craft knife) to accommodate a tongue on the leg. If a tongue is required on a modelled foot, build a piece of plywood into it for this purpose.

Insert the tongue into the slot and secure with a nail, ensuring that there is *some* ankle movement but insufficient to let the toes drag when the leg is lifted.

The design with the slot in the foot is recommended, as it permits you to exercise control more easily over the degree of ankle movement.

Latex-Rubber Feet

Rubber feet are cast in the same way as a rubber head (*see* Chapter 3). When making the plaster cast, insert the metal strips around the sole.

If the bottom of the leg is moulded with the foot, this may be fitted over the actual leg when attaching the foot. To secure it, push galvanized wire through both pieces at the ankle and bend the ends upwards. Ensure the lower leg that is moulded with the foot fits loosely over the leg to permit some movement, or the walking action may be impaired.

You may cast the parts with a tongue on the leg and a slot in the foot; insert the tongue in the slot and secure with a nail or piece of wire (*see* above). This will work only with fairly thick rubber; thin rubber will soon tear.

Alternatively, glue a rubber strip into a slot cut in the leg and insert the other end of the strip into the foot.

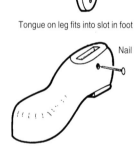

Tongue on leg fits into slot in foot

Nail

Fig 97 (b) the recommended ankle joint with the slot in the foot

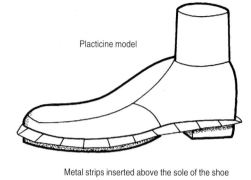

Placticine model

Metal strips inserted above the sole of the shoe

Fig 98 (a) Preparing to make a plaster cast for latex-rubber feet;

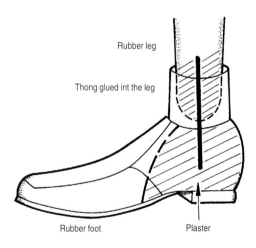

Rubber leg

Thong glued int the leg

Rubber foot

Plaster

Fig 98 (b) an ankle joint for latex-rubber puppets

Pour liquid plaster of Paris into the heel to hold the strip. You may pour a little also into the bottom of the leg by cutting a small slit in the calf.

COSTUME

Research costumes carefully and identify essential characteristics of a theme or period. Simple costume design that captures the essence of the line is usually the most effective, so do not let the design become too fussy or cluttered. You might reflect the shape of the puppet – or perhaps its head – in the costume, so that there is some unity to all aspects of your design.

If you make suits of clothes as you might for a doll, they are not likely to be successful and will probably restrict movement. It is usually more satisfactory to create the costume directly on the puppet, gluing or stitching as appropriate. Gluing tends to be quicker and leaves no seam edges inside the clothes to hinder movement; glued seams that are subject to strain will need a few stitches, however. The glue used depends on the material. Fabric adhesives are preferable, but clear, multi-purpose contact adhesive may be used for many materials.

To make a hem, smear glue sparingly but evenly along the edge, turn it up and press firmly. To make a seam, glue one edge and press it on top of the other. The glue prevents the outer edge fraying. Gluing is unsuitable for costumes with flowing robes and gathers, as it will stiffen the hem and prevent it falling in the desired folds.

Trousers are basically two tubes of cloth fastened together at the top. For a jacket, begin with the front and back panels, then add the sleeves, collar and lapels. A shirt under a jacket need only be a wide strip of material glued down

Fig 99 An array of costumes, using a wide variety of materials, on puppets from the Little Angel Theatre

Fig 100 Costume
construction

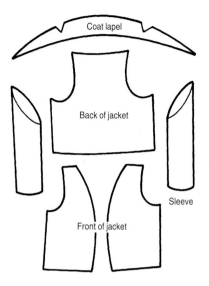

Back of jacket

Coat lapel

Sleeve

Front of jacket

Glue or stitch edges together

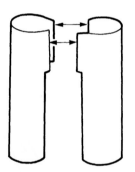

well; jersey fabric cut on the cross is particularly suitable for full, flowing robes.

When choosing a fabric, see how it hangs on the straight and on the cross, and try the right and wrong sides. Note differences in texture, and consider especially the appearance from a distance; use combinations of textures to achieve variety and set off one another. Puppets dressed only in jersey fabrics or in polyester cottons will not look very interesting.

Felt is useful for trimmings, but puppeteers hoard all manner of fringing, braids, ribbons, lace, fake fur, feathers, beads, costume jewellery, and so on, for their costumes.

The colours for a costume will depend on how suitable they are for the effect you want to achieve. Certain colours do tend to suggest particular characters or moods, but do not limit yourself to stereotyped conventions of colour symbolism; there are successful exceptions to most rules.

It is useful to consider the colour wheel showing primary and secondary colours, in order to achieve harmony in a costume. Having chosen one colour, look to the *analogous* colours (the neighbouring colours and the tertiary shades in between them), and also accentuate colours with a *complementary* colour (opposite your predominant colour on the colour wheel). Avoid combining complementaries in equal parts, as they will clash.

Try using nets and sheer fabrics over another material – for example, a pale voile over a deeper colour, or a dark lace over a vibrant colour. Try different shades of the same colour, contrasting colours, and the effects of a white overlay on darker colours.

While black works well for stage drapes, it is seldom successful for costumes as it tends to look flat; good

the front of the body, with a narrower strip around the neck for a collar. Period styles follow a similar process, with the shapes modified to achieve the intended line.

Dresses usually require front and back panels for the bodice, with sleeves added; the skirt may be cut in one piece or in a number of panels. Some costumes are created simply by draping, stitching and gluing a single piece of fabric on to the puppet.

Fabrics must stand up to wear but should be soft and fairly lightweight. If they are too heavy they hinder movement; if too thin, light shines through. They should also drape and move

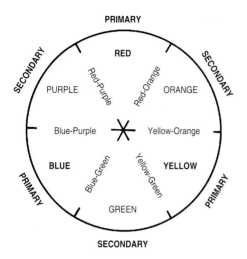

Fig 101 The colour wheel

substitutes are dark blue, dark green or dark brown.

Avoid large prints as these often look ludicrous on small puppets. Sometimes it will be necessary to stencil or paint a required pattern on a plain fabric – use textile paint or diluted acrylic paint. Despite the vast range of available fabrics, it is still difficult to find the right colour in the particular fabric, so it might be necessary to dye fabric. Always test a small piece of the fabric first; see how it looks when it is dry, as it is impossible to judge while it is wet. Dye the fabric before making it up into the costume and treat sufficient material to allow for errors in cutting and making up, as it is difficult to match colours with different batches of dye.

Coloured lighting has a tremendous influence on the colour of costumes so, when selecting the fabrics, consider the settings in which the character will

appear. You might be able to adjust the lighting a little, but not always enough to compensate for ill-chosen fabric colours. Try swatches of possible materials under stage lights before purchasing the fabric.

Fig 102 The Witch's costume used a variety of fabrics; from the Little Angel Theatre's production of *Rapunzel*

5 Control and Manipulation

This chapter details methods for constructing puppet controls, and techniques for operating each control. For further artistic aspects of manipulation, *see* Chapter 9.

GLOVE AND HAND PUPPETS

Control of a glove or hand puppet is essentially very simple although you will need a considerable amount of practice before you can achieve really convincing movements. Also needed is a good deal of stamina – holding puppets overhead for long periods of time is very tiring.

The Glove Puppet

This is best manipulated with two fingers in the neck. It is more comfortable than it appears and gives the most definite control of the head. To turn the head, press your first two fingers apart inside the neck, moving one backwards and the other one forwards to rotate the

Fig 103 A Polish glove puppet, with head modelled in paste and paper, in the Puppet Centre Collection. Note the fabric hands and the number of fingers, which is common with such hands

head. Manipulation with one finger in the neck is not recommended. It requires your whole hand – and therefore the whole puppet – to turn if the head is to turn, and the two fingers tucked into the palm can impede the handling of props.

Larry Engler and Carol Fijan (*Making Puppets Come Alive*, David and Charles, 1973) provide a useful introduction to glove puppet manipulation. They emphasize the importance of maintaining an upright posture and avoiding holding the puppet at an angle, or resting your arm or elbow against the stage. They suggest movements and gestures to practise, including trying with your finger movements to achieve convincing nodding, beckoning (motioning with a hand towards the body), waving, clapping, pointing, rubbing the hands together, tapping, thinking, creeping, crying, sneezing, and snoring. Add wrist movements and try bowing, looking or searching, reading, acting shy and sad, picking up an object, sitting down, sneezing, and snoring. With whole arm movements, practise walking, running, hopping, fainting, and falling. Then try a sequence, incorporating various combinations of these movements.

Hand and Mouth Puppets

Insert your whole hand in the head, with the thumb moving the lower jaw. Keep your wrist bent, otherwise the puppet will be looking upwards all the time; the audience should be able to see its eyes. If using your own hand for the puppet's hand, try to refine hand and arm gestures while keeping this arm close to the puppet. Sometimes the costume for the arm and hand is pinned or sewn to the body of the puppet to prevent it 'wandering away' in error.

With such puppets you need to spend time working on ways of synchronizing mouth movements to speech. Do not just open and close the mouth by snapping fingers and thumb up and down – yapping – but use the action and position of the wrist to give life to the head. For example, as the mouth opens, the wrist moves slightly forwards, returning as the mouth closes. Do not open and close the mouth continuously while that puppet is speaking, and do not move it to every syllable of speech: match the mouth movement to the spoken word, opening the mouth on 'open' words, and note the amount of space needed between the lips for different words. Aim for clean and crisp mouth movement and, once you have mastered this, try to combine mouth movements with general movements and moods, as outlined above.

ROD PUPPET CONTROLS

The main feature of a rod puppet control is the central rod that supports the figure and is integral to the method of construction. Additional controls are added as necessary, to move the head, the hands, and, occasionally, the legs.

The Central Control Rod

After many years of experimentation with different methods of supporting the rod puppet and effecting head movements, many puppeteers have come to the same conclusion as John Wright (*Rod, Shadow and Glove Puppets from the Little Angel Theatre*, Hale, 1986). According to him, there is one simple method (*see* over) that is the most effective for the main control. It is used to support the puppet and effect all head movements.

Fig 104 (a) The recommended method for glove puppet manipulation;

Fig 104 (b) a common, but much more limited, manipulation technique

Fig 105 Manipulation of a hand or mouth puppet, keeping the wrist bent to prevent the puppet from permanently gazing upwards

To aid handling, you may glue the rod and bind it with thick cord at the point where you would normally hold it.

A TURNING HEAD

A central rod is attached to the head; the shoulder block (or whole body) is free to move on this rod, supported by a wooden collar. Turning the rod turns the head. While there may be a slight tendency for the shoulder block/body to turn too, it is possible to exert a significant degree of control over the body, and counteract this tendency by the control of the hands and arms via the hand control wires.

Fig 106 A central control rod with a supporting collar to hold the shoulder block permits turning

A NODDING HEAD

In order to make the puppet look up and down, the head pivots on the top of the central rod. Attach at the back of the head a pull-string, counterbalanced by the weight of the puppet's head. If necessary, attach a spring or strong rubber band between the front of the head and the control rod to pull it forwards.

Groove the central rod for the string, which runs through small screw-eyes and inside the supporting collar to a large curtain ring. Hold the control with one hand, using your thumb to pull the ring downwards. If you need to operate facing the puppet rather than from behind it, use your index finger for the nodding control.

Some puppeteers prefer to use a length of stiff wire (such as strong galvanized wire) rather than a pull-string; this allows you to put and hold the head in the required position more directly, but it is a somewhat more complicated method. The wire runs in the grooved rod and is secured by staples. The top of the wire is angled and made into an elongated loop; another piece of wire passes through this loop and is secured near the back of the head. Some adjustment to the angle of the control wire may be necessary in order to achieve smooth movement. The lower end of the wire is bent into a thumb rest to effect control.

A NODDING AND TURNING HEAD

Puppeteers use all manner of complicated arrangements for effecting turning via a control wire used for nodding. However, there is much to commend the simplicity of combining the turning and nodding methods described, especially using the pull-string method for the nodding component.

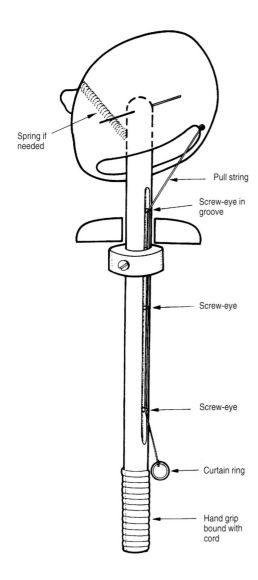

Spring if needed

Pull string

Screw-eye in groove

Screw-eye

Screw-eye

Curtain ring

Hand grip bound with cord

Fig 107 (a) The control method with a pull-string. This arrangement permits both nodding and turning;

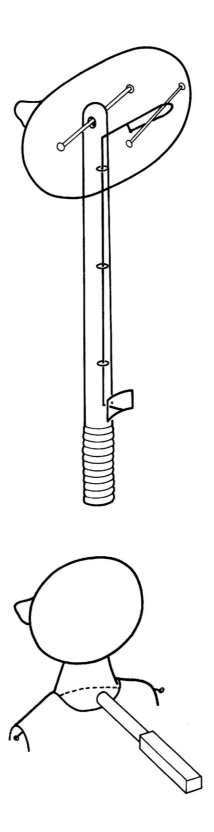

Fig 107 (b) a wire control for a nodding movement;

Fig 107 (c) a cord neck joint and a short rod to the neck, a method suitable for rod puppets held in front of the puppeteer

Figures with a cord neck joint (as in Fig 64(e)) are best operated from behind by means of a short rod secured in the back of the neck. Use either a wooden dowel or a strong metal rod. Glue it securely into a wooden handle of square-section wood, as this is easier to manipulate than a round rod.

Controlling the Hands and Legs

CONSTRUCTING THE CONTROL FOR HANDS

The hands may be controlled with thick galvanized wire or, preferably, stiff steel wire. Cut two pieces of dowelling, each approximately 12cm (5in) long. Drill a hole into the end of each dowel and glue the wires into the holes. These dowel handles facilitate control.

Make a small loop in the top end of the galvanized wire or, with steel wire, make a loop with soft but strong wire glued on with Araldite. Then attach the wire loops to the hands with thread through a hole in the palm. With some hand materials it is necessary to glue into the hand a small disc of wood for a secure fastening. It can be covered with whatever is used to cover the hand.

If you need more restricted hand movement, make a slot in the side of the hand, insert the rod and secure it with a nail through the hand.

If the hand is attached to the arm without a flexible wrist joint, an alternative method is to drill a hole through the arm, push the wire through, and bend the end over.

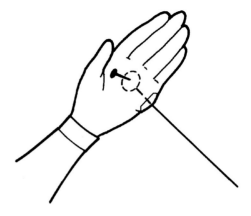

Fig 108 (b) wire secured in a slot in the hand;

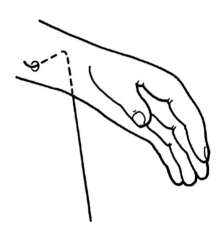

Fig 108 (c) wire attached to the wrist

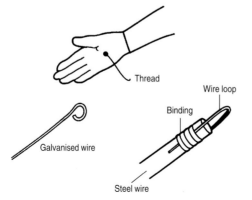

Fig 108 Fixing a control for the hands – (a) wire attached by thread;

CONTROLLING THE LEGS

Very often the legs dangle loosely. If, however, a leg control is required, attach screw-eyes to the tops of the legs (pivoted on a wire, as described on page 71), and tie thread to the screw-eyes. Attach the other end of the threads to a dowel rod which is paddled to produce a walking movement.

A much wider range of leg movements can be achieved with two-person puppets; a dowel rod, usually painted black, is glued into each foot, and the second operator effects leg movement by holding these. Alternatively, a bracket or strong steel wire in an inverted L-shape is secured in the back of the leg above the heel, and held by the second operator to move the legs and feet. These methods are more common with *Bunraku*-style puppets and 'black light' techniques.

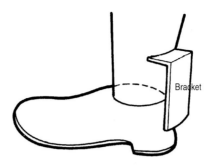

Fig 109 (c) an inverted L-shaped bracket or steel wire control

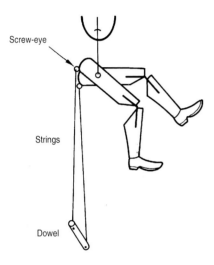

Fig 109 (a) Leg control strings for a rod puppet;

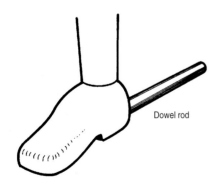

Fig 109 (b) a dowelling control for legs;

Rod Puppet Combinations

HAND-ROD PUPPETS

Insert your hand into the puppet's head, with your thumb moving the lower jaw. Control the arms with strong wires to the hands, attached as described above, and operated with your free hand.

ROD-HAND PUPPETS

The rod-hand puppet has a central control rod as described above; your own costumed hand and arm become the puppet's hand and arm.

ROD-GLOVE PUPPETS

The head is secured to a central rod as described above. Insert your thumb and index finger into the glove cuffs to control the hands; hold and turn the rod with your other three fingers.

ROD PUPPET MANIPULATION

It is not good technique to let one arm of the puppet hang limp while the

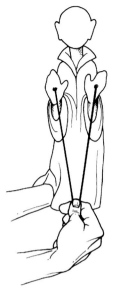

Fig 110 (a) The recommended operating technique for rod puppets: one hand holds the rod, the other controls both hand wires;

other is being manipulated. Preferably, hold the central rod with one hand and the two hand wires with the other. When holding the hand wires, you can hold them closely together, or in a slight V-shape with the thumb used to spread them, or spread wide with your thumb and index finger hooked around the two wires.

Occasionally, you might need to hold one of the wires with the little finger of the hand that holds the central rod, leaving your other hand free to control the other hand wire.

MARIONETTE CONTROLS

Strings attached to the puppet are joined to a wooden control that is constructed and manipulated in such a way as to produce movement of a particular part of the puppet. Measurements quoted here for controls are a guide only. They will necessarily vary with the size of the puppet.

This section describes first the construction of controls, then the actual stringing procedure, and finally manipulation technique. Dress the marionette before you string it.

Two kinds of marionette control are in common use: the upright control, and the horizontal or 'aeroplane' control. The tendency in Britain is to use the upright control for human puppets and the horizontal control for animals, but in some countries the horizontal control is used extensively for both. Many puppeteers claim to achieve a wider range of expressive movement with an upright control, and reserve use of the horizontal control for specialized applications such as the representation of a weight-lifter, an acrobat or a trapeze artist. The determining factor must be the requirements of the individual puppet.

Fig 110 (b) manipulation of hand wires to bring the puppet's hands together;

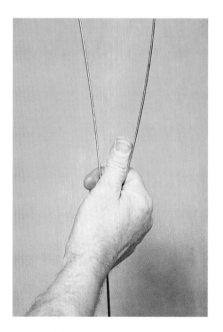

Fig 110 (c) spreading the puppet's hands a little;

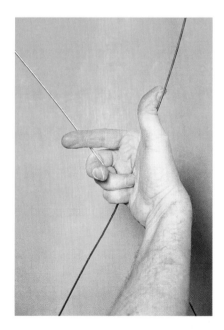

Fig 110 (d) achieving wide hand gestures

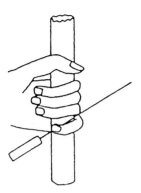

Fig 110 (e) holding the central rod and one hand rod together to leave your other hand free to operate a single hand wire

It is generally a mistake to make the control of a marionette too simple. Most strings support the puppet, and tilting or turning the control achieves a wide range of movements; if the control is too simple, it becomes more difficult to operate the puppet as the puppeteer must then pull individual strings to effect such movements.

As a rule, small holes are drilled in the control for the strings, the strings being threaded through and tied. Some puppeteers prefer to fasten screw-eyes for the strings, but this is not recommended as they tend to catch in the strings of other puppets. It is a good idea also to use the edge of a triangular file to make a groove around all bars where a thread is to be attached. This assists in securing the strings.

After construction, finely sand the whole control smooth before stringing – rough or sharp edges can damage the strings. If you are to perform in view of the audience, paint the controls matt black.

The Upright Control

The upright control consists of a vertical 22.5cm (9in) length of wood, to which a head bar is fixed, forming an inverted cross shape. To the back of the control is secured a shoulder bar. A detachable leg bar is suspended near the top of the control and wires to control the hands are attached to the main control just below the leg bar.

The main cross is made from 25 × 25mm (1 × 1in) wood, the leg and shoulder bars from dowelling 8-10mm (⅜in) in diameter, and the hand controls from galvanized wire.

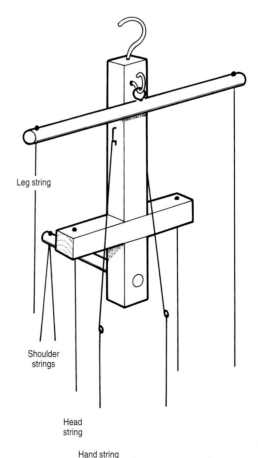

Leg string

Shoulder strings

Head string

Hand string

Fig 111 The upright control – (a) the basic control and stringing;

Attach the head bar (which should be a little longer than the width of the puppet's head), with a cross-halving joint. Make two saw-cuts half-way through each piece of wood and then chisel out the waste so that the two pieces can be glued and interlocked, and screwed together if necessary.

To attach the dowelling shoulder bar, drill a hole in the control (from back to front), below the head bar, and glue the dowel (about 12cm/5in long) into the hole, so that it sticks out at the back. Secure it further with a small nail. This dowel must be a tight fit and long enough to hold the shoulder strings away from the head so that its movement is not restricted.

Alternatively, the shoulder bar can be made of galvanized wire, which has the advantage that it can be folded for packing. To attach the wire to the control, first drill a hole through the main bar just below the head bar. Loop the wire through the hole, bend the ends together, and glue and bind together the two halves of the wire with strong thread. Bend the ends of the wire into a loop for attaching the shoulder strings. If necessary, to keep the shoulder strings well clear of the head, attach them to the ends of a separate dowel and suspend the dowel by a curtain ring from the loop in the end of the wire.

To attach the leg bar, screw a screw-eye into the centre of a dowel (about 20cm/8in long) and suspend this from the top of the control by a small hook.

Drill two holes, one about 8mm (⅜in) above the other, across the control for the hand wires, just far enough below the leg bar not to interfere with it. To attach the hand wires, first bend one end of each wire into a right-angle using pliers. Insert the long straight pieces of the wire through the holes in opposite directions, then carefully bend them over with pliers. Do not make them too tight to the upright or they will not turn freely; make the angles as sharp as possible, as wide curves will let them wobble. To obtain a sharp angle, while bending the wire down, keep a firm pressure upwards on the wire across the control. This takes a little practice to achieve.

Cut the wires to the same length and make loops in the ends for attaching hand strings; seal the closures of the loops with glue. These wires must be sufficiently long to rest on the head bar, and are usually about level with the bottom of the control.

If the puppet has mouth and eye strings, attach them to the ends of short dowels. To attach the dowels to the control, drill two holes in the front of the control above the head bar and glue the dowels into the holes.

Any back string may be attached to some part of the shoulder bar.

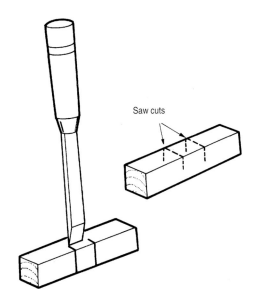

Fig 111 (b) making a cross-halving joint;

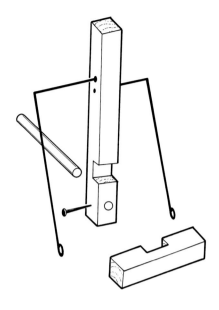

Fig 111 (c) an exploded view of the main control;

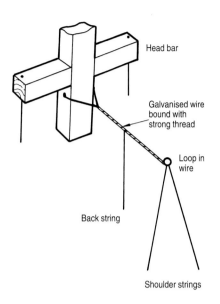

Head bar

Galvanised wire bound with strong thread

Loop in wire

Back string

Shoulder strings

Fig 111 (d) a shoulder bar that folds up for packing;

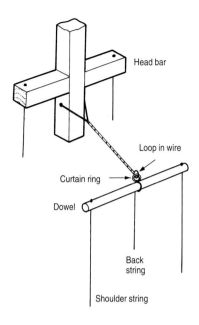

Head bar

Loop in wire

Curtain ring

Dowel

Back string

Shoulder string

Fig 111 (e) holding the shoulder strings away from the head;

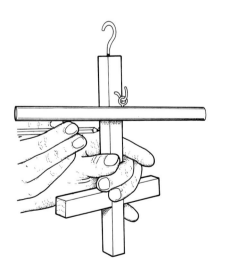

Fig 111 (f) marking the position for attaching the hand wires;

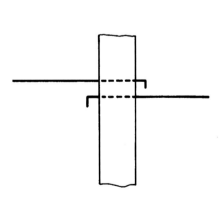

Fig 111 (g) the top ends of the hand wires inserted in the main control;

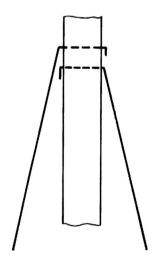

Fig 111 (h) the hand wires bent into position;

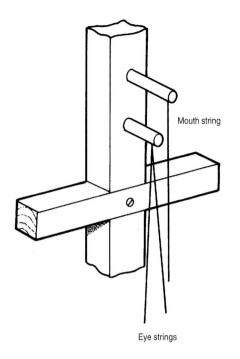

Fig 111 (i) fixtures for mouth and eye strings;

Screw into the top of the control a large hook for hanging it up. Some performers prefer thick galvanized wire bent into a large loop: the straight end runs down the control, is bent at right-angles to pass through a hole in the control, and is then bent at right-angles up the front of the control. Hammer the wire flat against the control, then glue and bind it with strong thread. The advantages of having a large wire hook are that it is easy to hang the puppet up in a hurry in subdued lighting, and it can be hung over many sizes of bar, and it can also hook on to your hand if the control is dropped; the disadvantage is that there is an increased risk of it catching in something.

A ROCKING BAR

A wooden leg bar screwed to the main control permits the control to be held and the puppet to be walked with one hand, leaving the other hand free. However, the leg action is not usually as good as when a separate leg bar is used.

Drill two holes through the leg bar and push the ends of a loop of wire through the holes. Bend over the ends of the wire, then glue and bind them

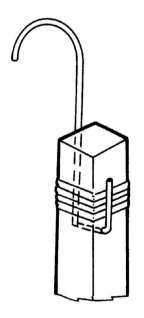

Fig 111 (j) a strong galvanized wire loop as an alternative to a large screw-hook

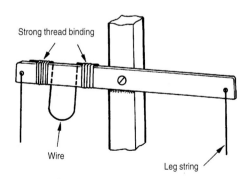

Fig 112 (a) A wooden rocking bar with a wire thumb loop;

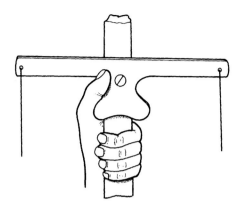

Fig 112 (b) a shaped wooden rocking bar

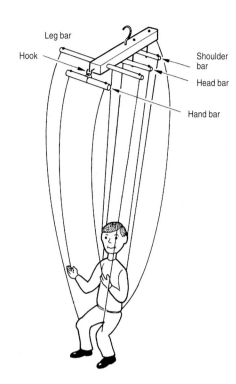

Fig 113 The horizontal control –
(a) the standard control and stringing;

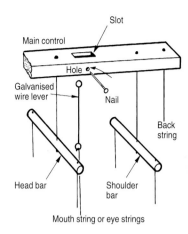

Fig 113 (b) attaching head
and shoulder bars and
controlling eye or mouth
movements;

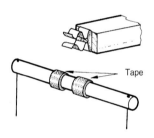

Fig 113 (c) a spring clip
used to hold the hand bar;

with strong thread. Slip your thumb into this wire loop to move the bar. Alternatively, use a strong plywood leg bar with two large notches cut out for your thumb.

The Horizontal Control

This control consists of a 20cm (8in) main bar of 25 × 25mm/1 × 1in wood, from which are suspended dowelling head and shoulder bars, and a removable hand bar. A leg bar is secured to the control, forming a T-shape. All dowels are approximately 7-10mm (¼-⅜in) diameter.

To attach the head bar, drill a hole down through the main bar, approximately in the middle, and another through the centre of the head bar. Thread cord through the holes and knot the ends. Suspend the shoulder bar from the back of the control in the same manner.

To attach the leg bar to the front of the control, glue the dowel into a hole drilled across the main bar.

To attach the hand bar, tie a small curtain ring to the dowel. Screw a small hook into the front end of the main bar and hang the hand bar from it. Alternatively, use a screw-on spring clip (a 'terry clip') to hold the bar.

To attach a back string, drill a hole down through the rear end of the control.

If the puppet is to have a moving mouth (or eyes), the string for operating this is controlled by a wire lever attached to the main control. Make the lever from a piece of 12- or 14-gauge galvanized wire, with each end bent into a loop. Cut a slot in the control just behind the head bar (drill a series of touching holes and clean the slot with a chisel or craft knife), and fix the lever in the slot by a nail through one of the loops. The mouth string (or eye strings) is tied to the other loop.

Add a hook for hanging up the puppet.

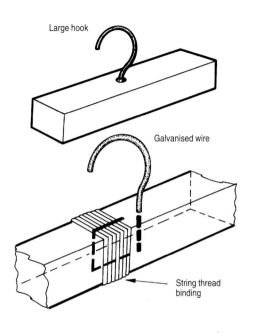

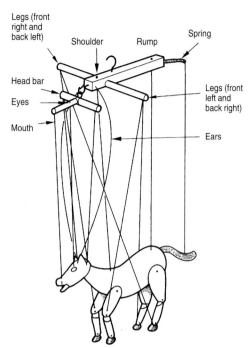

Fig 113 (d) a large screw-hook or a strong wire hook for hanging up the puppet

Fig 114 The horizontal control for animal marionettes

The Horizontal Control for Animals

This control has a main wooden bar (25 × 25mm/1 × 1in) about the same length as the puppet, with a dowelling leg bar attached at the front, as described for the previous control. A removable T-shaped head bar is suspended from the front of the main bar, and a spring (for example, a piece of curtain wire) to control the tail is attached to the rear of the control. Back strings are attached directly to the main control bar.

To make the head bar, drill a hole in the centre of a 12-13mm (½in) diameter dowel and glue into it a 5-6mm (approximately ¼in) diameter dowel. Attach the main head strings to the ends of the larger dowel. Attach a string to the nose, or to a moving mouth, to the end of the smaller dowel. To attach the head bar to the control, screw a hook into the front of the main control and suspend the head bar from it by means of a small curtain ring tied to the bar.

To attach back strings, drill a small hole down through each end of the main bar. Thread the strings directly through these holes, and tie them to the main bar. To attach the tail control, drill a hole into the end of the main bar and glue the spring into the hole.

For most animals, each front leg is connected to the leg bar at the same point as the opposite back leg, so that the puppet lifts these two legs together – front right and back left; front left and back right. Some animals, however, move their same-side legs together, which produces a rather rolling gait.

Add ear and eye strings if required. *Either* thread them through holes drilled in the head bar and knot them, *or* thread them through holes drilled across the front of the main control bar. If either of the strings is attached to the main bar, the ears will be raised or the eyes closed whenever the head bar is unhooked and lowered.

Add a hook for hanging up the puppet.

Stringing the Marionette

To string the puppet, use black Dacron braided nylon fishing line (strength 10lb), or a comparable substitute. Rub the thread with beeswax from time to time to prolong its life. Do not use nylon strings that are clear and shiny; they have a tendency to stretch, to glisten under stage lighting, and to retain crinkles after being wound up for packing.

The strings must be attached securely to the puppet, not to the costume or body padding. When attaching the strings to the control, wind them around the grooves filed in the bars; knot them loosely at first, so that adjustments can be made. The strings should be long enough to allow the control to be held comfortably over the back cloth (usually at about elbow height) when the puppet is standing on the stage.

With any removable control bars, such as a leg bar, make the strings just long enough to allow the bar to be unhooked without moving the puppet.

It is easiest to string a puppet when it is supported in a standing position. The best way is to stand the puppet on a table or a workbench and suspend it from a 'gallows'.

MAKING A GALLOWS

All you need is a suitable length of chain, and a hook from which to suspend it, so that you can hang the puppet from the chain at an appropriate height while it stands on a firm surface.

However, it is better to make a gallows that has a 1.5-1.8m (5-6ft) upright of 50 × 25mm (2 × 1in) wood held firm on a work table by three shelf brackets. At the top of the upright, attach at right-angles another piece about 30cm (12in) long, using a shelf bracket. Screw a hook for the chain into the end of this horizontal bar.

If you use two overlapping pieces of wood for the upright, joined by bolts with wing nuts and with equally spaced holes in each piece, you can adjust its height.

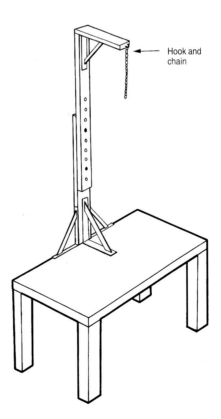

Hook and chain

Fig 115 A gallows for stringing marionettes

ATTACHING THE STRINGS

The procedure for stringing the puppet is as follows:

1. attach the head strings (with an animal, the back strings), so that the control is the required height. To attach the head strings, *either* drill small holes for the strings through the tops of the ears if they are strong enough, *or* fasten screw-eyes into a dowel built into the head (*see* Chapter 4);

2. using a needle to pass the thread through the costume, attach the shoulder strings (with an animal, the head strings) and back string, *either* to screw-eyes fastened in solid bodies, *or* thread the strings directly through holes drilled in the body. For bodies with a plywood centre, attach the strings to this; for hollow bodies, tie the string to a button inside the body;

3. attach the other ends of the threads to the shoulder bar. Adjust the tension of the head and shoulder strings so that the head is held in the right position in relation to the body. The back string should be a little loose so that it does not restrict body movement;

4. attach the hand strings – the position for the hole in the hands will depend on how you want the hand to be held. For example, you might drill through the back of the hand, through the thumb, or between the knuckles of thumb and index finger. With a larger drill bit, countersink the hole (to hide the knot). Thread the strings directly through the holes and knot the ends of the strings. Tie the other end of each string through the loop in the appropriate hand control wire. Make the hand strings just long enough for the puppet's hands to hang loosely by its sides when the hand wires rest on the head bar; they should not be slack;

5. attach the leg strings. Drill holes in the legs just above the knees; use a needle to insert the thread through the costume and through the holes in the legs, then knot the thread, ensuring that the knot does not impede knee movement. The needle needs to enter the costume just above the holes drilled in the legs: ensure that the costume does not pull or pucker when upward tension is applied to the thread. Attach the other ends of the threads to the leg bar; make the strings just long enough to permit you to unhook the bar without moving the legs;

6. having attached the main strings, attach any other strings that may be required. When all adjustments are complete, tie all the knots securely and seal them with a clear contact adhesive. Trim the ends of the threads close to the knots to neaten them.

MARIONETTE MANIPULATION

Here are three important pieces of advice about handling marionettes:

1. If a marionette is dropped off-stage, the golden rule is, do not just pick it up, as any loose tangles will be pulled into tight knots. Lift the control (not the puppet) gently, undoing the loose tangles carefully by tracing the strings up from the body in a sys-

tematic manner, twisting or turning the control as appropriate.

2. To prevent tangling when transporting marionettes, wind the strings round 'winders', rectangles of hardboard or plywood in which two slots have been cut to take the string; smooth the winders with glasspaper before use.

3. When puppets are not in use, keep them in bags made of strong fabric (for example, calico), which are large enough to allow the puppets to stand upright. Secure the bag with a draw-cord or tape inserted in the top hem. This helps to keep the puppets clean and to avoid damage.

The Upright Control

Hold the main control in one hand, taking the weight of the puppet with your middle, ring and little fingers. Position your little finger under the head bar if this is comfortable; otherwise, position it above the bar.

Use your thumb and index finger to move the hand wires and your free hand to unhook and operate the leg bar. While holding the leg bar against your palm (with your thumb, ring and little fingers), you can also use your index and middle fingers of this hand to move individual hand strings into positions not possible through operating the hand wires.

To nod or bow the head, tilt the control forward. To incline the head to one side, tilt the control sideways. This will not affect the movement of the shoulders.

To turn the head, tilt the control very slightly forward to take the weight on the shoulder strings, at the same time turning the control.

Fig 117 Manipulating the upright control: while the left hand holds the main control and operates the hand wires, the right hand operates the leg bar. Note how the fingers of the right hand are also used for more refined operation of the hand strings. Practice such manipulation with the controls in either hand

To bow the body and head, pull the back string taut to take the weight and tilt and lower the control. To bow the body while keeping the head upright, pull the back string taut and lower the control, keeping it upright so that the head strings are taut and the shoulder strings loose.

To walk the puppet, unhook the leg bar and move it in a paddling motion with your free hand. If you hold the control too high, the legs will swing in the air, if too low the puppet will walk in a sitting position. With practice you will come to feel when the puppet is just touching the floor because it will feel very slightly lighter. Keep the main control moving in unison with the leg movements. Try to achieve a rhythm in the movement of the main control as the puppet walks and use the natural momentum in the movement of the legs.

To make the marionette sit convincingly, first tilt the control slightly forward. If the puppet has a back string, pull this taut and lower the control a

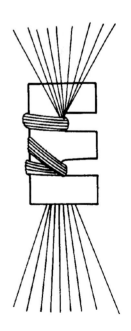

Fig 116 A winder used when transporting marionettes

little, as well as tilting it. Keeping the body bent forward, bend the knees and lower the body on to the chair. Finally, straighten up the control. To make it stand up again, lean the body forward before raising the puppet; observe how humans maintain balance while sitting down and standing up.

If the puppet has moving eyes or mouth, you can operate these in two ways: move the strings either with your free hand (which holds the leg bar), or by flicking out one of the fingers that hold the control.

Manipulating the Horizontal Control

Hold the control with one hand. To turn the head, tilt the control very slightly forwards to take the weight on the shoulder bar, and turn the head bar with your free hand.

To incline the head to one side, tilt the head bar sideways. To nod or bow the head, lift the shoulder bar with your free hand, or pull the string by which it is suspended with one of the fingers with which you are holding the control. At the same time, lower the control slightly, taking care to keep it level.

To bow the body and the head, tilt the control forwards. To bow the body, keeping the head upright, tilt the control and lift the head bar.

To move the hands, you may hold and move the hand bar in your free hand, but you may find it more effective to operate the actual strings with your free hand.

To walk the puppet, rock the main control from side to side in a paddling

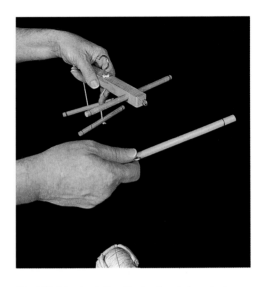

Fig 118 Manipulating the horizontal control

motion. The head and shoulders will remain level as they are suspended from the control.

To lower the puppet on to one knee, lift one leg string forwards with your free hand while lowering the main control and moving it slightly forwards.

To make the puppet sit, first tilt the control so that it leans forwards. Then bend the knees and lower the puppet to the chair. Finally, straighten the control.

Manipulating the Horizontal Control for Animals

Hold the control with one hand. To move the head, unhook the head bar and move it with your free hand. To effect movements of the body, tilt and turn the main control. To walk the puppet, rock the control from side to side.

6 The Shadow Puppet

PRINCIPLES

Shadow puppets are normally flat cut-out figures that are illuminated while held against a translucent screen. The audience on the other side of the screen watches the shadows created. Traditionally made of parchment or hide, they are now usually made of strong card or thin plywood, sometimes of translucent acetate, and occasionally wire, but there is scope for experimentation with all manner of materials. They are not difficult to make, and can look surprisingly delicate and intricate on the screen. (A related type of translucent, full-colour figure tends to be categorized together with shadow puppets, although it does not really cast shadows.)

Shadow puppets are controlled from below or behind, usually by means of wires or rods. It is common practice to support and move the figure by one main wire. Extra wires or strings may be added in order to effect particular movements.

The convention is to represent the figures partly in profile, partly straight on, which translates effectively on the shadow screen. The Javanese *wayang kulit* figures, for example, are designed with the head and legs depicted as a side view, while the body is viewed from the front. Slightly turning the body helps characterization.

When designing shadow puppets, plan their size in relation to the screen on which they will be used. Try to avoid very narrow parts, otherwise the puppets will soon break, unless they are reinforced or made of strong material.

For advice on lighting for shadow puppets, *see* Chapter 8.

Fig 119 A Javanese *wayang kulit* shadow puppet

CONSTRUCTION

For black silhouette puppets you can use fairly stiff, smooth card; black card is best, but a cereal box will do and is about the right thickness – use it with the plain side towards the screen, or paint it black. You may strengthen the card by coating it with PVA medium. A figure may be made from a number of

95

Fig 120 Mr Punch as a shadow puppet, cut by Lotte Reiniger, who made the first-ever full-length animated film. The design was a scribbled shape and the detail was achieved by cutting with small surgical scissors with short blades and long handles. The whole process took only a few minutes

different materials, for example, a loosely woven or stretchy fabric. Such puppets allow you to experiment with both texture and movement.

For medium to large figures that will have to withstand the rigours of a touring show, or that will be subjected to heavy use, use three-ply wood.

Simple Shadow Puppets

Design the figure on paper; then transfer your design on to a piece of cardboard. Cut out the shape with sharp scissors and add a control (*see* below).

Alternatively, transfer the design to thin plywood and cut out the shape with a coping saw or fret-saw.

Articulated Shadow Puppets

Design the figure on paper. There are no restrictions on where to make joints; it depends on what you want to achieve and what is practical. Often, parts move naturally without extra controls; those that need a separate control have to be held and operated, and you have only two hands. Moving mouths are possible if essential, but generally are best avoided – not only do they require a hand to control, but synchronization to speech is difficult to achieve and will distract the operator from the overall movement of the puppet.

Where the joints are to occur, draw clearly the overlapping parts. Transfer the design to a second sheet of paper, drawing all parts of the figure separately; cut out the parts as paper templates. Draw around the templates on to suitable cardboard, then cut out the separate parts with sharp scissors.

Join the parts, either with fine cord or with rivet-type paper fasteners as described below. When arranging the

parts for joining, step them one on top of the other. Do not join them in a fashion that will cause them to catch together while in use.

If you are using cord for joints, rub it with beeswax before use to prevent fraying. Dacron braided nylon fishing line is excellent for such joints even without waxing. Thread the cord through a suitable needle and push it through the centre point of the overlapping parts. Knot the cord on each side of the joint, close enough to the card to achieve a fairly tight joint, but not so tight as to prevent free, smooth movement. Seal the knots with a clear contact glue.

If you are using rivet-type paper fasteners, select ones that are not too long, but ensure that the heads are large enough not to go through the holes to be made for the joints. Use a paper punch to make a clean hole at the

Fig 121 (a) Designing an articulated shadow puppet;

Fig 121 (b) the first overlapping design is translated into a design in which all parts are shown separately;

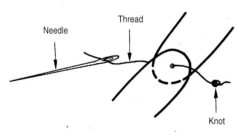

Fig 121 (c) a thread joint;

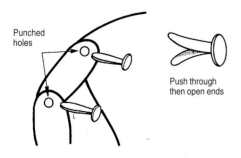

Fig 121 (d) a paper-fastener joint

centre point of the overlapping parts. A single hole punch is recommended, so that you can select the hole size; a simple stationery punch might also make holes too near the edge of the card.

Assemble the parts and, if the puppet is always to face one way, insert the paper fasteners with the heads on the side that is to face the screen. Open the split ends of the fasteners and press them down as flat as possible without restricting movement. If the ends are too long and show outside the puppet's profile, bend the points back towards the centre. Press the points in well to prevent snagging.

To restrict the movement of joints, link the moving parts with thread that is just long enough to permit the desired movement.

Card washers between the moving parts are sometimes thought to give greater flexibility. However, provided smooth card and good-quality thread are used, a washer should not be needed. Avoid anything that will prevent the puppet being held closely against the screen.

If you choose to cut the figure from thin plywood, you need to drill small holes and use cord to effect the joints. Knot the cord on the rear of the puppet. Such a knot would be too large on the screen side; instead, fray the end and glue it securely and as flat as possible on this side. It also might be secured with a staple gun. Check the security of the cord before each use.

Decoration and Colour

Design can be enhanced by cutting or punching shapes in the puppet. The Javanese *wayang kulit* shadow puppets, the Indian shadows and the beautiful, intricate, Chinese shadow puppets all use such methods, and it would help

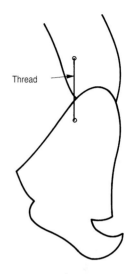

Fig 122 String used to restrict movement

Fig 123 *Shadow Fantasy* by the Little Angel Theatre: the figures, designed and made by Lyndie Wright, are cut from plywood and the cut-out shapes filled with cinemoid (stage lighting acetate) and textured fabrics

you to study these. How much it is possible to cut away depends on the material used; you must be careful not to weaken the figure.

If a design is cut in an articulated figure, avoid cutting away the overlapping parts. Leave sufficient material in both parts to allow the usual joint to be made.

Card figures with cut-away design may be strengthened by gluing a piece of clear acetate over any weak part. Alternatively, spray the entire puppet and press it on to a strong acetate sheet. Then cut out the acetate around the outline of the figure.

As an alternative to cutting an intricate design, you may cut away an entire area and cover it with an appropriate loose-weave textured material such as lace, net, and so on.

Colour can be introduced by covering cut-out shapes in puppets or scenery with coloured acetate, tissue paper or cellophane paper. Alternatively, puppets and scenery may be cut from fairly thick plain or coloured acetate. Plain acetate may be coloured with glass-painting colours or with

shapes cut from a self-adhesive, translucent, coloured film. This permits many colours to be combined in the same figure. Join moving parts with strong thread or with nylon thread, and seal the knots with a clear glue.

Fig 124 Shadow puppets designed and made by Lyndie Wright for *Peer Gynt*: the figures are painted with French Enamel Varnish on clear plastic which is sufficiently rigid to stand up without support but able to be cut with scissors. A Little Angel Theatre production

For a combined coloured and textured effect, coloured translucent materials can be used in conjunction with textured materials, and with black paint of a type suitable for the materials being used.

Three-Dimensional Puppets

Three-dimensional objects and figures permit exploration of the 'puppets' as seen from various angles. Solid objects with perspex or acetate parts have interesting properties, and shadow play using three-dimensional wire puppets also has possibilities.

Make wire figures from chicken wire or by bending galvanized wire to the required shapes. Join separate parts by interlocking small loops made in the wire. Control the figures with wires in the same way as you do a rod puppet.

Solid, three-dimensional puppets with strong designs can be used to

good effect to cast two-dimensional shadows; for example, characters may appear at one time as rod puppets and at another simply as shadows. As a three-dimensional puppet cannot be held flat against the screen, a strong, single source of light, such as a projector, is needed.

Tricks and Transformations

Solid black figures are able to 'hide' features, so that a puppet can be unfolded, or a hidden part rotated into view, to transform the character.

Back-projected scenery can be similarly transformed. The two interlocked scenes in Fig 126(b) permit a change of scene in silhouette. The structure, attached to a rod, must be held securely by a small shelf or some other device in front of the projection unit. It is rotated to transform one image into another.

You may want your shadow figure to have a variety of expressive hand gestures. To achieve this, cut out substitute hands and arms, mount them on a wire or strip of strong acetate, and hold them in place. The arm that is attached to the puppet must hang completely out of sight.

Full-Colour Puppets in the Traditional Style

Full-colour puppets can be created easily, using techniques akin to those of the traditional oriental puppets, but with modern materials. The technique of making the puppet from lampshade parchment and tinting it with inks has been used to good effect for some time; alternatively, you can colour plain card and treat it with oil to make it translucent. The best card to use is Ivory

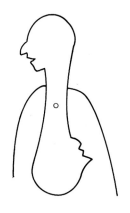

Fig 126 (a) A transformation shadow puppet;

Fig 126 (b) transformation scenery

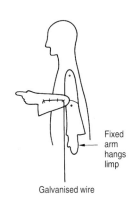

Fixed arm hangs limp

Galvanised wire

Fig 127 A substitute hand

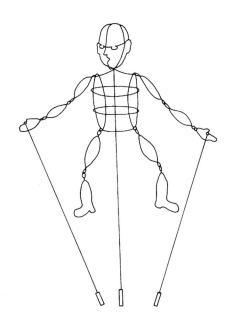

Fig 125 A three-dimensional, wire-sculpture shadow puppet

Fig 128(a) Shadow puppets by Christopher Leith for his own production of *Jack and the Beanstalk.* The puppets are made from lampshade parchment, tinted with coloured inks.

Board and the best weight is 335g per square metre for figures up to 60cm (24in) high; otherwise use 400gsm.

For colouring, felt-tip pens are satisfactory: water-based pens are preferable, as the colours are stable and will not merge. With spirit-based pens the colours drift together; for a few weeks the effect is subtle and beautiful, but eventually the colours may merge and spoil the effect. Watercolours and transparent dyes, diluted and painted on, are better. 'Dylon' is one possibility; Luma Water Colours or, preferably, Dr Martin's Radiant Concentrated Water Colours are recommended. With Dr Martin's, a great deal can be achieved by diluting in different strengths and by mixing just three colours – Turquoise Blue, Daffodil Yellow and Tropic Pink.

First, design the puppet and transfer the design lightly on to thin white card;

remember to allow for the overlaps if it is to be jointed. Do not cut out the separate parts at this stage. Next, colour the puppet with your chosen form of transparent colouring; colour the side that is to face the screen, as this helps the colour to show with the maximum intensity. Ensure that you completely fill in blocks of colour; light shading is not effective.

Carry out the following process before doing any cutting out of the shape or detail.

To make the card translucent, lay it on a piece of paper towel on a protected work surface. Rub the coloured card with a piece of paper towel soaked in either cooking oil or, preferably, clear liquid paraffin, which is cleaner. Use enough liquid to soak into the card effectively, but do not flood it. Rub it in well. Then rub oil or paraffin into the other side of the card until all the colour shows through (the card will now be translucent and stronger). Hold the card up to the light; any areas not sufficiently covered will appear darker and slightly grey.

Wipe any excess liquid from the card with a clean sheet of paper towel and finally cut out the shape and any required detail. Do this last, to avoid damage to the puppet while applying the oil or paraffin. If you have any fragile parts, such as a walking stick or a tail, you may leave white card between this and the main part of the puppet; provided it is well treated, the white area will scarcely show.

If the puppet is jointed, use nylon thread (4lb fishing line is suitable) to join the parts, as described on page 96; seal the knots in the thread with clear glue. Gluing the knot to an acetate washer on each side of the card joint prevents the knot pulling through the card. Instead of a knot, the thread may be melted to a tiny bobble at each end

Fig 128(b) The Ringmaster by Jessica Souhami: the puppets, made from Ivory Board, are coloured, then oiled to make them translucent. The controls are 12- or 14-gauge piano wire

with a lighted spill. Small, rivet-type paper fasteners may be used for joints, but they will show on the screen.

For strengthening, coat the puppet with PVA, carefully covering one colour at a time to avoid smudging. This creates a hard plastic finish. Alternatively, clear acetate may be sewn or stapled to any weak part. It may be glued with UHU if all excess oil is removed, but will hold only temporarily.

Store the puppets in polythene bags to protect your clothing, to stop them sticking together, and to prevent them drying out; if they do dry out, they will need to be re-treated very carefully with oil or paraffin.

CONTROL

Principles

It is common practice to attach controls to the body (or to the head, if it moves), and to one arm, if needed. The other arm and legs are allowed to swing freely. In fact, considerable control can be exercised indirectly over the puppet's legs from one main control rod or wire.

For the control, use 12- or 14-gauge piano wire (from model shops), galvanized wire (coat-hanger wire) of a gauge that will remain straight under the weight of the puppet, or 8-9mm (⅓in) diameter softwood dowel. Garden canes and the like are usually unsuitable. When using wire, it is useful to glue the end into a dowel rod for easier

Fig 129 A nylon thread joint

Figs 130 (a) and (b) Effecting shadow puppet movement via a single control rod

handling (a long wire with a short rod, or a short wire and a long rod). Make the hole for the wire a very tight fit and ease the wire in with pliers.

The controls illustrated here will meet most needs, whether the puppet is operated from below or behind. The puppet may have a head *and* body control, but this is more difficult to operate. Restrict controls to the minimum necessary to achieve the desired effect, and certainly do not have more than you can hold. Let the puppet's natural movements and the audience's imagination supply the rest; the merest hint of movement is sufficient.

With simple table-top shadow theatres, control from behind is favoured. This will give you comfortable operation and flexibility of movement, although your position will depend also on the mode of lighting – the operator cannot stand between the light and the puppet. For larger presentations, operation from below screen level is preferred, with the control at an angle of about 45 degrees to the puppet. For this reason, the method of control shown in Fig 131(a) is recommended, as it permits operation from any angle, as well as providing very direct control of the puppet.

Methods of Fixing Main Controls

If the puppet has a moving head, the main control is fixed to the head. If it does not, hold the puppet loosely between your thumb and forefinger, and adjust the position to find the point of balance. Attach the main control to the body just above this point so that there is *just a little* more weight below the control than there is above it. The puppet will now remain naturally upright, rather than trying to 'somersault' as you operate it. Use one of the following techniques to attach the control; the first two are the recommended methods.

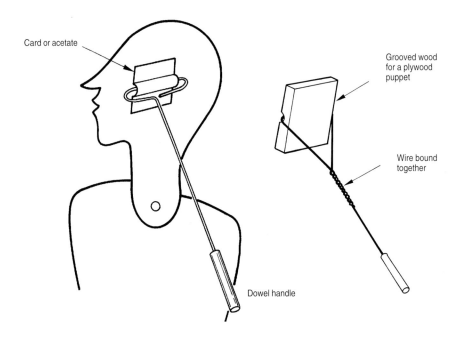

Card or acetate

Grooved wood for a plywood puppet

Wire bound together

Dowel handle

Fig 131 Methods of fixing a head control – (a) a wire control joined by card or by a small wooden block;

1. Wire with an elongated loop in the end may be secured by a strip of card (or acetate) glued to the puppet over the wire, but not to the wire itself, so that the wire can be raised and lowered for control from any angle.

2. The same principle may be used with a plywood puppet. Use thicker wire and secure the loop with a grooved piece of wood glued on to the plywood with the wire turning freely in the groove. The end of the wire loop may need to be bound securely to the main shaft of the wire.

3. Secure the rod to the puppet with a drawing pin (thumb-tack). It must be tapped in firmly, or the puppet will turn on the rod. This is suitable only for horizontal controls.

4. Glue Velcro (spikey surface) tape to the rod and (fuzzy surface) to the puppet (use UHU glue for oiled puppets). For extra security, staple the Velcro to the puppet. Velcro is suitable for puppets up to about 30cm (12in) high; larger puppets will be too heavy. This is suitable only for horizontal controls.

5. Fix a large eyelet in the puppet and attach a rod by a toggle pushed through the hole. The toggle, made from a small piece of dowel, is attached to the rod by fairly thin but strong wire. This method permits control from any angle.

6. A small loop in the end of a control wire may be sewn on to a suitable point at the edge of the puppet. This permits control from any angle and also allows the puppet to be turned round to face the opposite direction, but control is less definite.

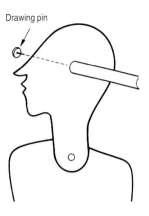

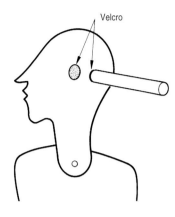

Fig 131 (b) a rod secured with a drawing pin;

Fig 131 (c) a rod secured with Velcro;

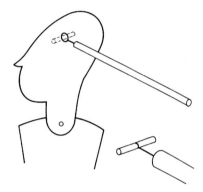

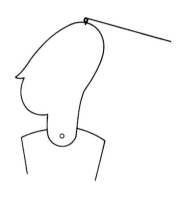

Fig 131 (d) an eyelet and toggle fastening;

Fig 131 (e) a loop in the wire sewn to the puppet

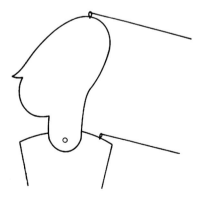

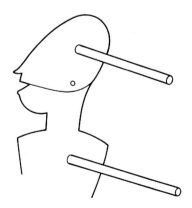

Fig 132 (a) Effecting head or mouth movements from behind;

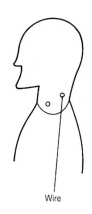

Fig 132 (b) a head
controlled from below

Clearly, using only the last of these methods it is possible to turn the puppet to face the opposite way. However, with shadow puppets it is an easy task to make a duplicate facing the other way. When deciding which side to attach the controls, take account of who has to talk to whom, and what the action requires.

Controlling Moving Heads and Mouths

When a moving head is needed, it is often manipulated by attaching the main control to it rather than to the body, and a certain amount of control may be exercised over the body with a little practice. Alternatively, the puppet may have the main control attached to the body, and a second rod or wire attached to the head to effect head or mouth movements (*see* Fig 132(a)).

Fig 133 A moving mouth on a Thai shadow puppet

Another possible method, which is not so satisfactory, controls the moving part by a piece of stiff wire attached where good leverage can be achieved. A main control to the body is also required.

A pull-thread to the mouth can be used to open it, while a strong rubber band returns it to the closed position.

Arm Controls

It is possible not to have any arm controls, and to let the arms hang and move freely. With the very large Indian figures, it is common practice for the puppeteer to pick up the hand and simply hold it against the screen.

The best all-purpose method for controlling arms from behind or below uses galvanized wire. Make a loop in the end of a piece of wire; seal the closure of the loop with glue. Use strong thread to tie the wire to the hand to be controlled. Umbrella spokes are useful alternatives for this control.

Other methods for control from below use acetate or string. Attach a strip of strong, clear acetate to the hand using thread knotted at each end, as for arm and leg joints. Alternatively, extend the top of the arm to give a little

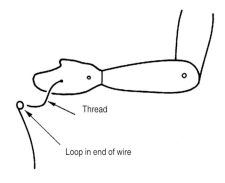

Fig 134 Fixing controls for arm movement –
(a) a wire control;

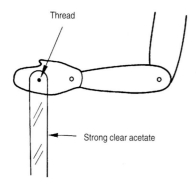

Fig 134 (b) an acetate control;

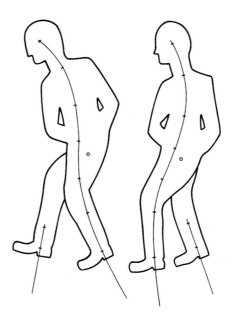

Fig 134(d) Articulate one
of the puppet's legs in
order to achieve a
controlled walking action

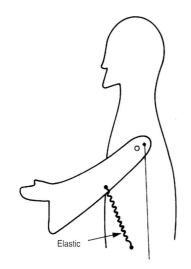

Fig 134 (c) a string control

leverage and attach a string. Pull the string to raise the arm. For more controlled movement, you can attach a piece of elastic to the arm and body to provide a counter-pull to the string.

Leg Control

The best advice on leg controls is not to use any. Movement is invariably better when the legs hang and move freely. It is possible to effect satisfactory leg movements through the main control rod, with a gentle swinging or rocking motion and slight downward pressure.

If it is essential to move a leg in a particular way, attach a piece of galvanized wire or a strip of strong, clear acetate, joined to the foot with thread.

If a controlled walking action is required, cut out the figure with one leg articulated. Attach the main control wire to the figure and an extra wire to the articulated leg. As it walks, the puppet stoops forward slightly and then straightens up.

7 Staging Techniques

STAGING PRINCIPLES

No single puppet stage will suit all performances or all venues. If one stage is needed for all performances, compromise – in both staging and performances – will be necessary. However, the basic stages or staging units described here can be adapted to meet a range of requirements.

Any stage should be presentable, portable, strong and rigid, easy to assemble and dismantle. It must accommodate the performers and their equipment comfortably, and must meet performance needs: the puppets need space to act, otherwise they will be lined up along the front of the stage. For larger stages, adjustable width and height – and possibly depth – are helpful, because of the idiosyncrasies of

Fig 135 (a) Visibility angles created by a proscenium arch;

Fig 135 (b) glove or rod puppets disappear from view if the audience is too close;

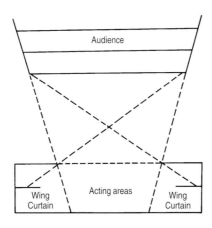
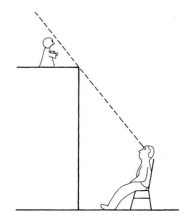

Fig 135 (c) sight-line problems occur if marionettes are too low;

Fig 135 (d) a raised stage with a raked auditorium or tiered seating

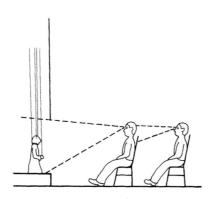
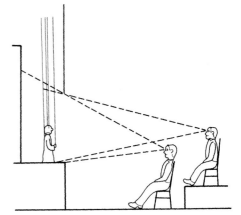

Fig 136 (a) *Love for Three Oranges*

Fig 136 (b) *Just So Stories*

Fig 136 (c) *The Firebird*

Fig 136 (d) *Two Magic Oxen*

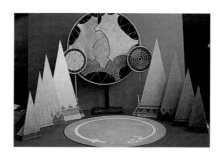

Fig 136 (e) *Hiawatha*

Fig 136 (f) *La Boite et Joujoux*

different venues. Sight-lines are important, too; open stages permit a wider viewing angle than a proscenium theatre, which limits the spread of an audience and the size of the visible acting area.

For comfortable manipulation, the front curtain of a glove- or rod-puppet booth should be just above the puppeteers' heads. Therefore, spectators sitting too close to the fit-up might have a restricted view of glove or rod puppets as soon as they move away from the playboard.

Visibility problems arise also if marionettes are too low or the audience is too close. Keep a marionette stage well above floor level. The ideal is a raised stage floor and a raked auditorium or tiered seating, but there must be enough headroom for the operators.

While the units described form the basis for many forms of presentation,

do not consider staging simply in terms of a conventional booth. Variations are possible, so above all be creative with the space in which you work.

GENERAL STAGING STRUCTURES

Simple Staging: A Table-Top Theatre

A table-top theatre may be used with all types of puppet. Dimensions will depend upon your transport facilities and the number of puppeteers, but a recommended minimum screen size is 100cm wide by 70cm high (40 × 28in). Use 50 × 25mm (2 × 1in) timber, approximately 9mm (⅜in) diameter dowelling and 18mm (¾in) chipboard.

Figs 136 Scale-model designs for stage settings in a variety of styles, by John Blundall

Use wood-working glue as the adhesive.

An exploded view of the parts is shown in Fig 137(a). The frame is four lengths of timber, glued and screwed together at right-angles with half-lap joints.

For the base, glue and screw two lengths of timber to the chipboard, taking care to countersink the holes for the screw-heads. Use the bottom of the frame to ensure that the timber is appropriately spaced. Insert the frame into the slot in the base. If necessary, secure it with bolts and wing-nuts.

Use another length of timber for a lower cross-bar. Drill a hole through each end of the cross-bar and the two uprights, then secure the cross-bar to the frame with bolts and wing-nuts after attaching the shadow screen to the frame. Secure the shadow screen (*see* page 132) tautly with drawing pins (thumb-tacks) to the top and sides of the frame. Bolt the lower cross-bar in

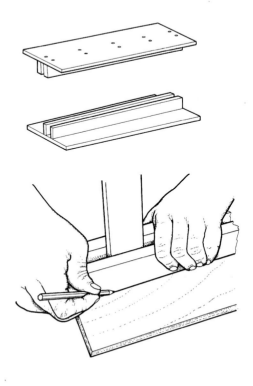

Fig 137 (b) the main frame for supporting the screen or backcloth;

place, pull the screen under it and pin it to the side facing the operator. This cross-bar provides a ledge on which shadow puppets walk, and the space between screen and cross-bar can hold scenery.

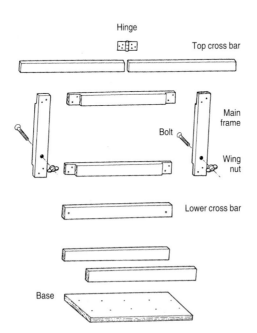

Fig 137 The table-top puppet theatre –
(a) an exploded view;

Fig 137 (c) the base of the theatre;

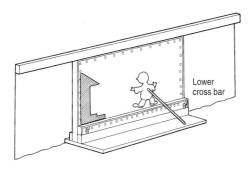

Fig 137 (d) attaching the screen and lower cross-bar; also shown is the top cross-bar supporting the front curtains, and the use of the screen for shadow puppets;

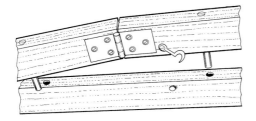

Fig 137 (e) attaching the top cross-bar with dowel pegs, which fit into holes in the main frame;

Fig 137 (f) the theatre used for glove or rod puppets;

The top cross-bar (for the curtain rail) is two lengths of timber, joined with a strong hinge. To attach this bar to the frame, use four 12mm (½in) diameter dowel pegs, each 7.5cm (3in) long. Clamp the cross-bar in position on top of the frame and drill four appropriately spaced holes down though the bar and frame. Glue the dowels into the holes in the bar so that they protrude downwards to fit into the holes in the frame. The cross-bar is held in place by its weight; a small hook may be used for extra security.

Curtains may be gathered and pinned in place on the cross-bar, or hung on a curtain wire or rail. A curtain rail with a cording set gives smooth operation for revealing and covering the shadow screen.

Open the curtains for shadow play. Close them for use with glove and rod puppets, or to give an open stage for marionettes.

A similar table-top stage can be made with aluminium square-section tubing, *see* page 113. It is quickly assembled and dismantled, conveniently reducing to a small pack of tubing. To make attaching curtains and a shadow screen easier, wooden battens are screwed to the tube with self-tapping screws.

Fig 137 (g) the theatre as an open stage for marionettes

Fig 138 (a) Dexion square-section aluminium tube used to create a table-top theatre. The pieces can be rearranged with other lengths of tubing into any shape required;

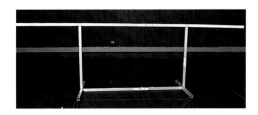

Fig 138 (b) the aluminium table-top theatre dismantled. The wooden battens attached to the tube facilitate the attachment of a shadow screen or curtains

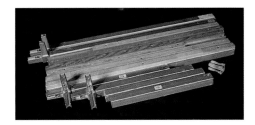

Flexible Staging Units

DESIGN

Many stages can be designed on a unit structure. Setting up with units is easier than bolting together and bracing many separate timbers, and a complete unit system gives great flexibility of

stage design. The units are constructed in a variety of shapes and sizes, but the use of standard sizes enables the units to be rearranged in different configurations. Some may be left as single units ('flats'), while others are hinged together ('book-flats'). They may be joined in any shape required. Depending on the mode of transport available (if they are to be toured), the units may conveniently be anything up to 2.5m (8ft) high. Design the structure so that weight is well distributed, and it cannot topple over. Stage weights may be used if needed.

Cover the frames either with drapes (which tie on to the frame with strong, fabric tapes), or with a suitable fabric stretched across one face and glued and stapled to the sides of the frames. Fabrics used range from hessian (burlap) to velvet. Alternatively, use one of the methods detailed on pages 126-127.

Screens for rear-projection or for shadow play may be built into the structure and a selection of arches, windows, turrets, and so on, may be built from 5-7mm (¼in) plywood on a timber frame, as needed.

All of the designs illustrated assemble or dismantle in minutes, and comprise the set of units shown in Fig 140(e).

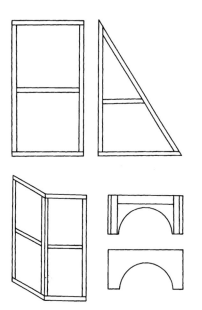

Fig 139 A variety of shapes for flexible staging units

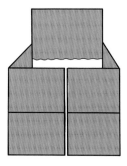

Fig 140 Staging units assembled in different formats – (a) a basic glove booth;

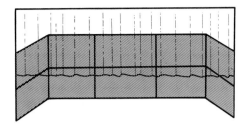

Fig 140 (b) the basic booth, extended by an additional section, for use with glove or rod puppets;

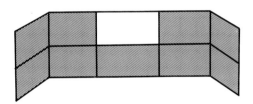

Fig 140 (c) a shadow screen introduced into the staging;

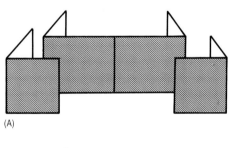

(A)

(B)

Fig 140 (d) a narrow (A) and an extended (B) open stage for marionettes;

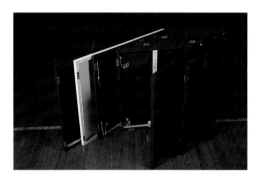

Fig 140 (e) the units for all the preceding arrangements dismantle into the selection of units shown here

As an alternative to these fixed units, square-section aluminium tube is excellent. It can be joined in an infinite number of shapes and rearranged as necessary using special corner joints (*see* page 113).

CONSTRUCTION WITH WOOD

Wood is used for most stage structures, but joints must be true and secure and the whole structure suitably braced to prevent wobbling; 50×25mm (2×1in) timber is suitable for many applications.

Glue and screw joints, using woodworking glue. Half-lap joints are recommended; if carefully cut and secured, they should not need bracing. If they do, glue and screw triangular wooden blocks into the corners.

For joining the units, pin-hinges are quick and easy to use. You can make them by knocking the joining rod out of a standard hinge and replacing it with a thick, galvanized-wire 'pin'. A strong method is bolts with wing-nuts, but they are fiddly, time-consuming and get lost; avoid drilling holes where they might weaken the timber, but drill any holes thoroughly so that the bolts fit cleanly without being loose.

Alternatively, dowel pegs glued into holes drilled in one section fit into corresponding holes drilled in the other section. The units are held in place by their own weight, or by hooks, or are

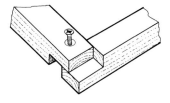

Fig 141 (a) Constructing a half-lap joint for the staging units;

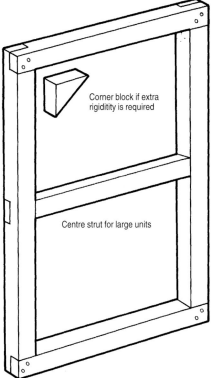

Corner block if extra rigiditity is required

Centre strut for large units

Fig 141 (b) the basic frame for each 'flat' may be braced with a central strut and corner blocks if necessary;

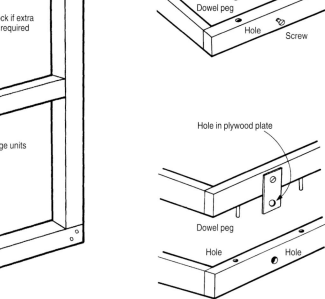

Slot in plywood plate

Dowel peg

Hole

Screw

Hole in plywood plate

Dowel peg

Hole

Hole

Fig 141 (d) joining two stage sections;

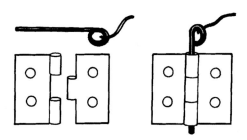

Fig 141 (c) a pin-hinge used for joining separate units. The hinges must be aligned very carefully on all units if they are to be interchangeable;

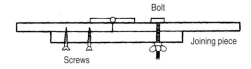

Bolt

Screws

Joining piece

Fig 141 (e) securing a hinged bar;

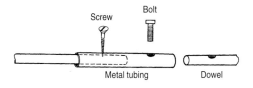

Screw

Bolt

Metal tubing

Dowel

Fig 141 (f) a metal tube used to join two large dowel rods

secured with a plywood or metal plate, which is screwed to one section and either bolted to the other section, or slotted over a screw in it.

A bar hinged for transporting may be held rigid by a length of wood, screwed to one half and bolted to the other. When thick dowel rods need to be joined, insert one dowel half-way into a length of metal tubing and secure with a screw; insert the second dowel into the other half of the tube, and secure it with a removable metal pin or bolt.

CONSTRUCTION WITH SQUARE-SECTION TUBING (DEXION)

Dexion square-section aluminium tubing is strong and light, easily cut to length and assembled with joining pieces in various shapes (*see* Figs 138(a) and (b)). The equivalent in steel (Dexion Speedframe) is even stronger, but much heavier and more difficult to cut.

Either material may be made up into rectangular unit structures, hinged, bolted or clamped together. The corner joints permit pieces of tube to be introduced or rearranged wherever required. To effect a joint, a plastic insert is placed in the end of the tube, the joining piece inserted and tapped firmly into place with a mallet; the next length of tube is then joined in the same way.

To reduce long pieces of tubing to manageable sizes for packing, use another square tube or U-section aluminium, the same size as the *internal* dimensions of the Dexion tube. Half of the internal tube fits into one section and is secured with self-tapping screws; the other half slots into the other section. With vertical tubes, gravity holds them in place; horizontal

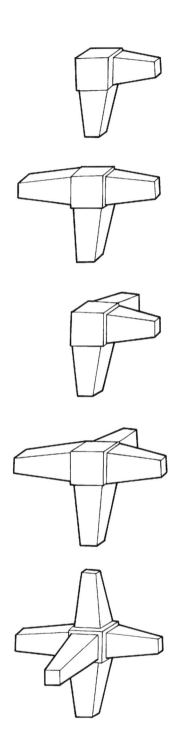

Fig 142 (a) A selection of joining pieces for square-section tubing;

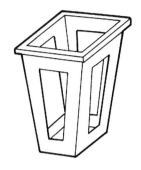

Fig 142 (b) a plastic insert used to secure the joints;

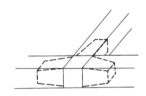

Fig 142 (c) sections of tubing joined together;

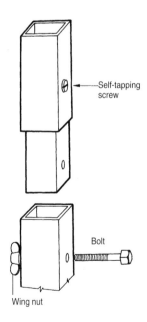

Fig 142 (d) joints in long bars to facilitate transportation

tubes require a bolt or some other metal pin to secure the internal tube.

Plywood shapes such as arches or turrets may be attached to the aluminium frame using self-tapping screws. Attach drapes with fabric tapes or, if they are not too heavy, with Velcro tape glued securely on to the tubing.

STAGES AND SCENERY FOR GLOVE, HAND AND ROD PUPPETS

Most glove or hand puppets are presented within a booth, usually without a proscenium arch. Rod puppets tend to be contained within a stage of larger proportions. Staging units may be adapted in a variety of ways. Fig 143 shows a booth in which two units are

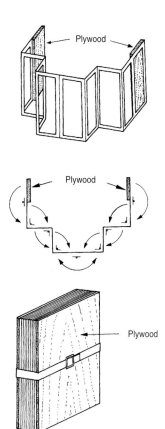

Fig 144 A basic frame, which folds up as shown to create a box for puppets, props or curtains

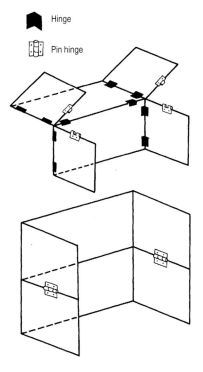

Fig 143 A staging unit secured with two pin-hinges

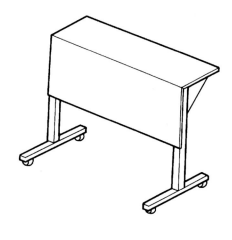

Fig 145 A playboard on casters

hinged horizontally: the upper unit is simply lifted into place and secured to the lower unit with two pin-hinges, one on each side. The two pins are pulled to dismantle the whole structure.

Hinged units may also be adapted to create boxes for carrying curtains, puppets, and so on. The units are hinged in a zig-zag arrangement so that they fold flat. Glue and screw a sheet of plywood to the outer sections of the folded frame, to create the box, which is secured with a strap.

The height of the booth depends upon the height of the puppeteers. It is best to perform standing, with the playboard just above your head. You might need to adjust the height for different venues, for example, in a steeply raked auditorium, where the back rows might be looking down into the booth.

Some performances without a booth will require a portable 'playboard', a surface on which to establish some of the action. A simple framework supporting a plywood playing surface is sufficient. It will need wheels or casters with a locking mechanism, or wheels at one end and blocks of wood at the other, to prevent it moving unintentionally. Cover the front surface with another sheet of plywood for a tidier appearance; this allows you to have a prop shelf below the playboard.

An Open Booth

In its simplest form, this fit-up consists of a front screen to hide the operators, and a back drop against which to operate the puppets (*see* Fig 140(a)). The suggested minimum width is 1.25m (4ft) but 1.5 to 1.8m (5-6ft) will serve solo performers well. For small group work with two or three puppeteers, a 2.5-3.5m (8-12ft) booth is recommended. Many performers work with a depth about half the total width, but two-thirds is a better proportion.

The main structure is book-flats, for which possible designs are small units with legs bolted on, small units on top of each other, or taller units. Those with legs allow finer height adjustment; those that stand directly on the floor tend to be more stable. It is also worth exploring the use of multiple acting levels.

Join the units with pin-hinges; insert additional flats to extend the stage, or to introduce a shadow screen. One or two extra sets of book-flats of different dimensions permit some height adjustment by adding to or replacing the existing units.

The back frame may be three lengths of timber, hinged or bolted together and bolted to the sides of the stage. Attach plain or scenic drapes or a back-screen (*see* pages 128-130).

Fig 146 (a) Example of structures for a basic open booth;

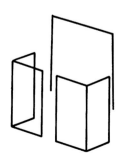
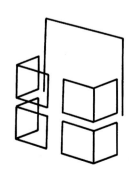

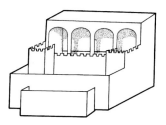

Fig 146 (b) alternative staging, providing multiple acting levels

When extending a booth with legs, bolt extra legs to the front centre section for extra support. To make legs adjustable, drill a series of equally spaced holes in the structure and the legs, so that the parts may be bolted together at different heights. To allow for changes in height, use a 'skirting' curtain at the bottom of the booth.

You may also need some of the accessories described opposite.

A Proscenium Booth

The main booth is the same as for an open booth, but it has an extra unit containing a plywood proscenium. Dimensions are similar, the width of the proscenium opening ranging from half the width of a large booth to two-thirds or more of a smaller booth. As a proscenium reduces the viewing angle, you need to keep the opening as wide as possible to allow scope for action.

Although this is not very desirable, the proscenium may be hinged in the centre. When in use it is held firm by a plywood plate on the inside; this is screwed to one half and hooks over a screw in the other half.

Accessories such as a playboard and prop shelves may be added, and slotted battens may be attached to the booth for supporting backcloths (*see* page 130). It is common for the fixed back-screen (preferably slanted) to be a sky-cloth.

If proscenium curtains are used (*see* page 127), ensure that they draw back completely behind the sides of the arch, or they will further limit the viewing angle. The opening may also accommodate a shadow screen.

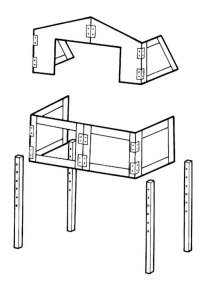

Fig 147 (b) the separate parts of the booth – one possible design;

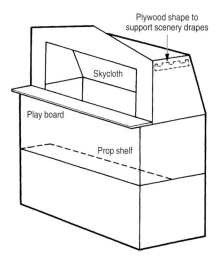

Plywood shape to support scenery drapes

Skycloth

Play board

Prop shelf

Fig 147 (a) A proscenium booth;

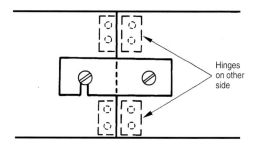

Hinges on other side

Fig 147 (c) securing a hinged proscenium

Accessories

PLAYBOARD

This is a front 'shelf' of approximately 10-15 × 2cm (4-6 × ¾in) timber upon which props may be stood; for props on rods, it must be slotted. Sand it very smooth and very slightly rounded at the edge on the operators' side, for operator comfort, and to reduce wear on costumes. Bolt the playboard on to the main frame. This may be used to adjust the width of a booth by acting as a bridge between two separate book-flats. It may be hinged for transporting. Small playboards can be attached where needed, to allow scenery to be attached (*see* page 119).

PROP SHELF

Prop shelves can be very handy. The shelf may be a length of plywood, like the playboard, but attached lower in the booth; alternatively, it may be made up of triangular plywood plates. In each case, cut the pieces to fit the cor-

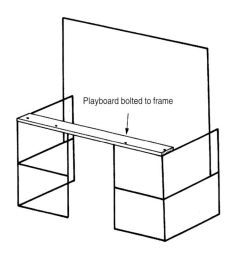

Fig 148 (b) a playboard bolted to the frame may be used to adjust the width of the staging;

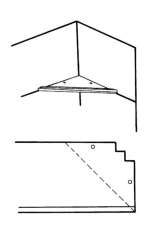

Fig 148 (c) a small corner prop shelf and one that fits full width. Both have the corners cut away to fit the staging;

ners of the booth. Both methods may be used to hold the framework rigid. It is a good idea to attach a strip of beading along the edge, to prevent props sliding off.

An alternative is a fabric cradle attached to two long battens, which bolt on to the framework. This method holds props more securely but does not aid the rigidity of the framework.

A HANGING-WIRE

This can be provided by a curtain wire fixed to the inside of the main frame. It is useful for hanging up glove puppets when they are not in use (*see* Fig 71(e)).

Fig 148 (d) a fabric cradle for props

Scenery

PLYWOOD CUT-OUT SCENERY

Scenery can be provided by a cut-out plywood shape, finished in relief if desired. To enable it to be attached quickly and easily, inverted keyhole

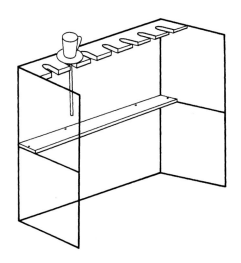

Fig 148 (a) A playboard, shown here slotted to accommodate props on rods;

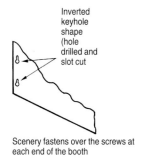

Inverted
keyhole
shape
(hole
drilled and
slot cut

Scenery fastens over the screws at
each end of the booth

Fig 149 Supporting cut-out
background scenery

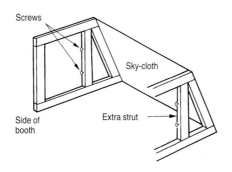

Screws

Sky-cloth

Side of
booth

Extra strut

shapes are cut in the plywood, which
fit over the heads of large screws in the
framework. Suspend a backcloth or
sky-cloth behind it.

THREE-DIMENSIONAL SCENERY

This is usually too cumbersome for
mobile puppeteers, but is ideal for a
group with a permanent base. It may be
made from plywood, polystyrene, cor-
rugated or smooth card, or even cardboard boxes. Ensure that the scenery
has a firm base or supporting structure
so that it cannot be knocked over. For
free-standing scenery in a booth, telescopic lighting stands or purpose-built
structures are used, but they must be
very stable, possibly held firmly by
stage weights.

SECURING SEPARATE ITEMS OF SCENERY

Cut-out scenery may be screwed to a
batten which bolts on to the stage.
Wooden blocks screwed to the framework help to secure it. Alternatively,
scenery may be glued and screwed to a
block of wood, and bolted or clamped
to the frame or the playboard.

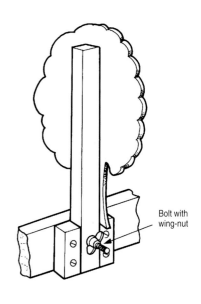

Bolt with
wing-nut

Fig 151 (a) Scenery bolted to the stage;

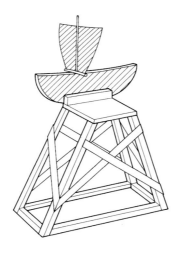

Fig 150 A purpose-built
structure for free-standing
scenery

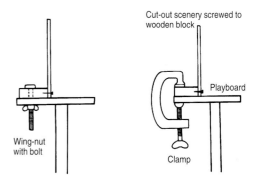

Cut-out scenery screwed to
wooden block

Playboard

Wing-nut
with bolt

Clamp

Fig 151 (b) scenery clamped or bolted to the
playboard

A SCENERY SLOT

Scenery constructed from plywood (or other suitable materials attached to a plywood strip) may be attached to a booth by the use of a scenery slot, made as follows:

1. Cut out the plywood shapes, leaving a strip (scenery tag) projecting downwards to fit into a slot in the booth.

2. Glue and screw three strips of plywood to the frame of the booth (*see* Fig 152(a), to create the slot.

3. Cut away the opposing piece of the frame to accommodate the scenery slot when the booth is folded up. Insert the scenery tag in the slot and drill a hole through the plywood, the tag and the framework.

4. Insert a dowel peg into the holes to secure the scenery in place. Attach the dowel to the frame with screw-eyes and thread.

Use this technique also to attach a 'scenery groundrow' to the booth.

A SLIDING SLOT FOR SCENERY

This permits scenery to be introduced smoothly during a performance, without the puppeteer's hands being seen.

The 'slide' is a length of timber attached vertically to the main frame, and the 'sliding slot' that holds the scenery consists of four small pieces of wood glued between three longer pieces to form two slots.

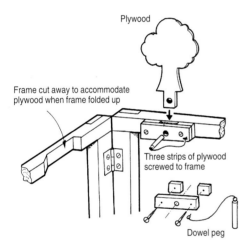

Fig 152 (a) A scenery slot;

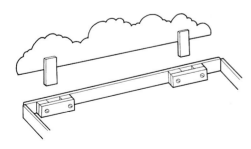

Fig 152 (b) a scenery groundrow, attached to the booth

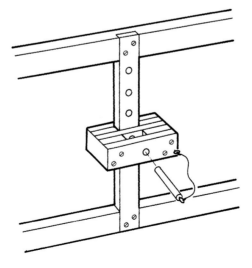

Fig 153 (a) A sliding slot for scenery;

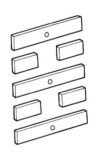

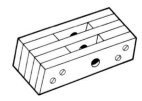

Fig 153 (b) the construction of the sliding slot, with spacers glued between the main strips;

Fig 153 (c) inserting the scenery into the slot, with a dowel peg used to hold the scenery at the required height;

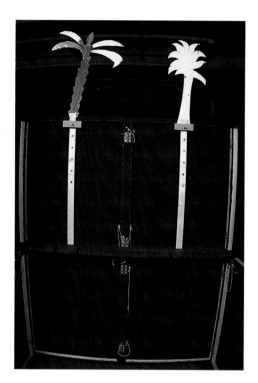

Fig 153 (d) a back-stage view of the scenery slot in use;

Fig 153 (e) the view from the audience

The vertical slide fits into one slot and the scenery tag into the other. The scenery tag is a block of wood, glued and screwed to the back of the scenery and projecting downwards. Insert the scenery, raise the slot to the top of the slide and drill a hole through the entire assembly to accommodate a dowel peg, which is used to secure the scenery in place. Drill a series of holes in the slide to permit the scenery to be held at different heights.

FASTENING PROPS

Props may need temporarily to be held securely in place; a spring clip, a large bulldog clip or Velcro tape may be used to hold the object on the playboard. Properties on rods need a slotted playboard.

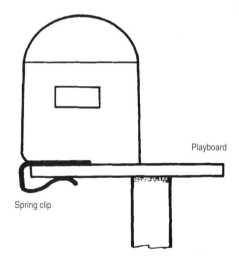

Playboard

Spring clip

Fig 154 The use of a spring-clip to hold properties on the playboard

STAGES AND SCENERY FOR MARIONETTES

Marionette presentations generally need to be raised, either by setting up on a platform, stage or rostra blocks, or by the use of a built-in feature of the puppet staging. Totally open-stage performing, in which the puppeteer appears fully visible on stage with the marionettes, is used most frequently for cabaret and variety acts. It provides greater scope for movement and action than the more traditional forms of presentation.

Most performers operate on a stage with a backcloth suspended from a cross-bar, known as a *leaning bar*, which is usually about waist-high to the puppeteer. It is desirable to have a stage floor covering, such as thin carpet, hessian (burlap), or felt, to provide a good surface for puppets to walk on without making too much noise. You also need a *perchery*, a hanging-rack for marionettes off-stage. You can build it on to the staging, or use a separate rack, such as a free-standing, easy-assembly clothes rail.

Staging

A FREE-STANDING BACKCLOTH FOR OPEN STAGING

This may be designed on a unit structure or from aluminium square tubing (*see* page 113). Alternatively, a simple leaning bar may be attached to supporting legs.

A BASIC OPEN STAGE

This type of stage has a backcloth, perchery, and wings to hide both backstage activity and puppets preparing to enter. Construct it from staging units with appropriate additions, from square-section tubing or from timber bolted together with suitable bracing.

AN ELABORATE OPEN FIT-UP

The stage has a raised stage floor and operating area, backcloth, wings, perchery, and a drape behind the puppeteers, to concentrate attention on the stage. The raised platforms must be secure and steady. You might design the operating bridge to be supported on

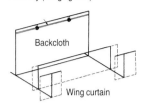

Fig 155 A simple open stage design with perchery and wings

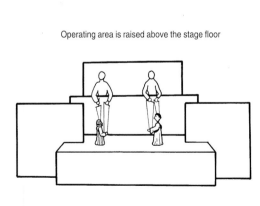

Operating area is raised above the stage floor

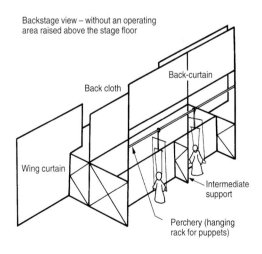

Backstage view – without an operating area raised above the stage floor

Back-curtain

Back cloth

Wing curtain

Intermediate support

Perchery (hanging rack for puppets)

Fig 156 A more elaborate open stage with a raised stage floor. The operating area may be on the same level or raised above the stage floor.

Fig 157 Portable proscenium stages – (a) stage with no bridge;

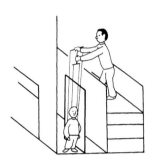

Fig 157 (b) a stage with a higher backcloth and a small bridge;

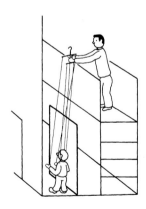

Fig 157 (c) a stage with a high bridge over the stage floor gives the stage area more depth, so puppets are not operated too close to background scenery;

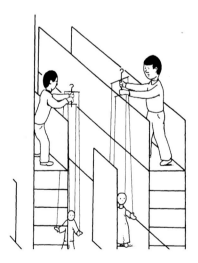

Fig 157 (d) high bridges above the stage floor, one over the proscenium opening and one over the backcloth

strong wooden boxes, used also for transporting puppets and equipment. The operating area may be higher than the stage floor if the puppets are large, or if you want to distance performers from the puppets.

Bolt the upright supports for the leaning bar, perchery and back drape on to the legs of the platforms. The perchery will probably need intermediate support. Design the back of the operating area so that the puppets can hang freely on the perchery.

Attach curtains or scenery to the leaning bar and to the wings (*see* page 126). A shadow screen may be incorporated in the structure below the leaning bar and covered with curtains or scenery when not required.

PORTABLE PROSCENIUM STAGE DESIGNS

Five types of proscenium stage are illustrated in Fig 157. The most elaborate will make great demands in terms of construction, weight, transport and

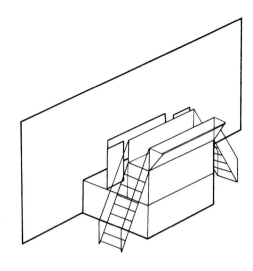

Fig 157 (e) an elevated proscenium stage

setting-up time. The simplest has a proscenium, stage floor, backcloth and usually wings.

A raised operating level is desirable. It raises the puppeteers and is essential where you would otherwise be visible to the audience through the proscenium opening. A deeper stage floor with a bridge, or bridges, over part of it creates a sense of greater depth, as the puppets no longer perform close to the backcloth. It also offers more scope for action.

Proscenium stages invariably need to be set up on a platform, or designed with an elevated structure.

A PROSCENIUM STAGE WITHOUT A BRIDGE

This is a framework of timber or square-section aluminium tube. The front curtain frame supports two rows of curtains, the top one overlapping the lower one by a few inches.

With the lower set open, the stage becomes a marionette stage; with the top set open, it is a glove or rod stage. A

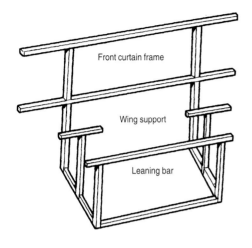

Fig 158 (a) Framework for a basic stage without a bridge;

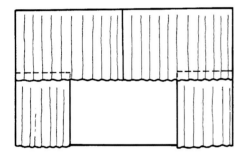

Fig 158 (b) the lower set of curtains open for marionettes;

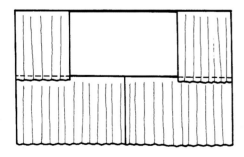

Fig 158 (c) the upper curtains open for glove, rod, or shadow puppets;

shadow screen may be fixed into the upper opening. For glove and rod puppets, raise the leaning bar/back-screen. Add wing curtains to conceal backstage activity.

Adjust the width of the acting area by varying the curtain opening. For curtain control, *see* the advice on proscenium curtains (page 127).

For a raised stage, the structure is essentially that of the elaborate open stage, with a frame to support proscenium curtains.

A PROSCENIUM STAGE WITH A BRIDGE

When a stage has a bridge, its construction must be very strong. The bridge is intended to increase depth so, within the acting area visible to the audience, there are no supporting pillars between the front of the bridge and the stage floor. Basically, two towers support the bridge. Therefore, the construction needs to use materials such as scaffolding poles or slotted metal angle, which is ideal but very heavy.

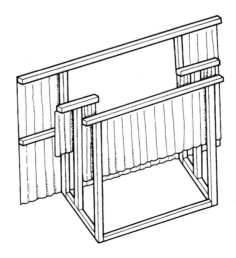

Fig 158 (d) a raised back-screen and wings, for use with glove and rod puppets

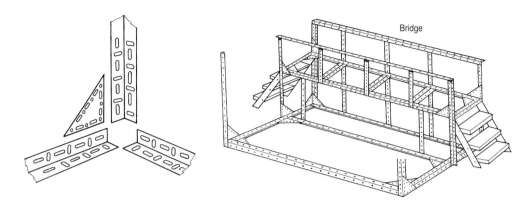

Fig 159 The stage and bridge area constructed from slotted metal angle, bolted together with large nuts and bolts, using spanners

Bridge

The design depends on individual needs, and different dimensions or weights to be supported will require different amounts of support or bracing with triangular plates or angle struts. The stage and bridge floors are strong plywood or chipboard, bolted on. For such a major undertaking, it is undoubtedly better to seek professional advice.

Accessories for Marionette Stages

ATTACHING RODS

To join metal tubing or dowelling rods to the main structure, towel- or wardrobe-rail holders are very useful.

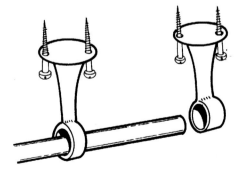

Fig 160 Towel- or wardrobe-rail holders used to carry dowels or metal tubing

A CLEARING ROD

A strip of plywood screwed to one end of a dowel rod is used to reach props on the stage during scene changes, or if anything is dropped!

A GALLOWS FOR THE STAGE

Gallows are used to suspend a puppet on stage, either if two hands are needed to manipulate a special effect, or if the puppet is on stage but not moving. Any form of projection with a length of chain or loop of cord will serve the purpose, but a hinged gallows is often preferred, as it can be pushed out of the way when it is not needed. The following are two methods for constructing gallows.

1. Bend a metal rod into a right-angle. Drill a hole in the end of a dowel rod, then glue one end of the rod and jam it into the hole. To strengthen the dowel, glue a sleeve of aluminium tubing over it. Use a screw or screw-eye to fasten a chain or cord to the other end of the dowel. Make a groove in a block of wood and screw the block to the stage wherever it is needed. The metal rod fits into, and turns in, the groove. Hook the puppet's control into a link in the chain or a loop in the cord.

2. Drill a hole in each of two strong, triangular plywood plates. Hinge the plates to the staging as required. Fit the ends of a strong dowel or aluminium tube into the holes in the blocks. In each end of the dowel, drill a hole to accommodate a bolt (to prevent the dowel coming out of the blocks). Suspend cords or chains from the rod.

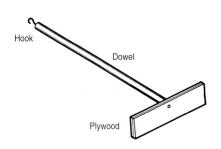

Fig 161 A clearing rod

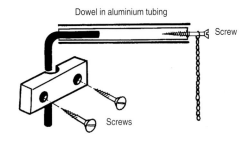

Fig 162 (a) Making a gallows for the stage;

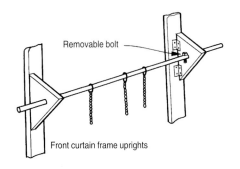

Fig 162 (b) a gallows for a large stage

Scenery

TWO- AND THREE-DIMENSIONAL SCENERY

The methods detailed for glove and rod puppets (*see* pages 117-118), and for back-screens with relief modelling (*see* page 129) may be used also for scenery for marionettes. It is essential that such scenery is secure. Attach it to the stage, to a large base board, or to a smaller base held firmly by stage weights.

AN INSET

This is used to screen off part of the stage. It may be made in the same way as staging units or from plywood or hardboard with strong linen hinges glued along the edges.

SCREEN SETS

These are flat cut-out shapes made into a three-dimensional background; finishing them in relief increases their effectiveness. Hang a backcloth behind the screen set; it is usually a fairly generalized scene of sky, or of a distant view.

STAGING FOR MIXED PUPPET PRODUCTIONS

When using marionettes and other types of puppet together, an open style of performance (*see* Fig 165(a)) will often offer a satisfactory solution for practical staging problems. However, Fig 165(b) demonstrates a very successful combination of glove puppets, rod puppets and marionettes within a more conventional setting.

Shadow puppets may be used with other puppets, either on the back-

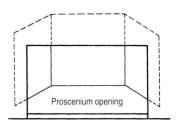

Fig 163 An inset, used to screen off part of the stage

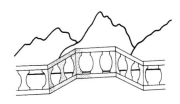

Fig 164 A screen set, creating a three-dimensional background

screen, or to the sides, or above or below the main acting area. Design the staging to incorporate the shadow screen with adequate room for operating the other puppets without impeding the lighting and manipulation of the shadows. A screen in a proscenium opening can be introduced and removed smoothly for a particular scene, but other types of puppet cannot be used simultaneously with this method.

CURTAINS AND BACKCLOTHS

Drapes for the Stage

Drapes should enhance the staging without attracting attention to themselves, and should be suitably lined or heavy enough to prevent light showing through. If flexible staging units are

Fig 165 (a) Mixed-puppet productions: *Starchild*, a rock-opera by Barry Smith's Theatre of Puppets, utilized open-stage methods to combine rod puppets, *Bunraku*-style rod puppets, marionettes and masked actors

Fig 165 (b) Mixed-puppet productions: The Mad Hatter's Tea Party from *Alice in Wonderland* by the DaSilva Puppet Company. Alice and the Hatter are marionettes, the Hare is a rod puppet, and the Dormouse is a glove puppet

permanently covered, they may not need separate drapes, but the covering fabric should be protected in transit.

Velcro tape (sewn along the curtain and glued and tacked or stapled to the framework) provides a quick and easy device for attaching drapes to the stage. For heavy drapes, *either* use heavy-duty press-studs (sewn on to the curtain and screwed to the stage), *or* stitch long loops of tape to the drapes at regular intervals, take these over the framework, and attach to hooks screwed inside the staging.

Proscenium Curtains

Draped curtains are not recommended for general use in puppet theatre, as they reduce considerably the size of the proscenium opening.

THE STRAIGHT CURTAIN

Hang two curtains from a corded, heavy-duty curtain track of the kind used for domestic purposes. Operate the curtain cords by hand or use a quiet-running, remote-controlled, motorized unit. Ensure the curtains pull back clear of the proscenium opening, or they will affect sight-lines.

THE PULL-UP CURTAIN

Tack the top of the curtain to a wooden batten. Fix two screw-eyes in the top of the batten, one at each end, and tie a cord to each screw-eye. Screw three pulleys into the upper cross bar, two directly above the screw-eyes in the batten, and the third wherever required to the side. Thread the cords over the three pulleys as illustrated (*see* Fig 166), and knot the ends of the cords together. Pulling the cords down raises the curtain. Screw hooks into the

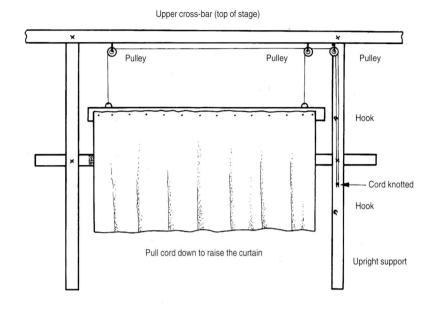

Fig 166 The pull-up curtain

upright support and loop the cord around the appropriate hook for the height required.

THE DROP CURTAIN

This curtain requires less height above the proscenium than the pull-up curtain. Tack the top of the curtain to a batten. Sew about four sets of curtain rings to the curtain in vertical rows.

Fig 167 The drop curtain

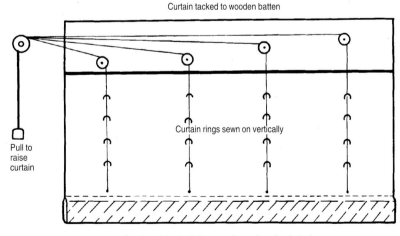

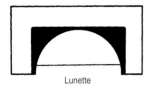

Lunette

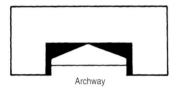

Archway

Fig 168 Lunette and archway masking drapes for a proscenium opening

Fig 169 A variety of stage sets designed by John Blundall. These illustrate well how sets can be appealing, yet not distract from, nor obscure any puppets that may be operated in front of them:

Thread cords through the rings and tie them to the lowest ring in each row. Screw four screw-eyes or pulley wheels to the batten directly above the cords, thread the cords through/over these, and then over another pulley at one end of the batten. Tie the cords together, so that when they are pulled they raise the curtain. Weight the curtain with a thin batten or dowel in the hem.

MASKING DRAPES FOR PROSCENIUM OPENINGS

The proscenium opening in the front curtain may be any size or shape required. The most popular all-purpose shape is the 'pageant' (or 'processional') opening, which is approximately twice as wide as it is high. To vary this, drapes may be suspended on a batten to mask the opening; 'lunette' and 'archway' styles are illustrated in Fig 168.

Backcloths and Back-Screens

Sets should be appealing, but not too 'busy' or bright, or they will be distracting or obscure the visibility of the puppets. The effectiveness of many designs is in their simplicity.

GAUZE

Suspend theatrical gauze across the stage and illuminate it in front with lights to the sides, not shining directly on to it; any scene painted on the gauze is visible to the audience, but objects and scenery behind are invisible. With lighting behind the gauze instead of in front, the scene previously invisible becomes visible and the scene on the gauze disappears.

A SOLID BACK-SCREEN

Glove and rod puppet stages often have a plywood back-screen with cut-out entrances, exits and windows. The shape and finish is often neutral; matt black is common, so that, with a little decoration, it may represent various settings. Alternatively, a scene may be painted on, or built up with relief modelling (*see* opposite), and then painted. Cover 'doors' and 'windows' with small curtains attached to the back of the board and either split down the centre, or secured at the top like a flap, to permit easy access but hiding any back-stage activity.

PLAIN DRAPES

For all types of three-dimensional puppet, a plain, draped curtain serves

(a) *The Voyages of Sinbad;*

(b) *The Quest For Olwen;*

(c) *Hansel and Gretel*

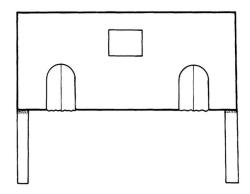

Fig 170 A plywood back-screen

many purposes. A fairly dark, neutral colour is usually preferred or have rails with three or four sets of drapes in different colours to open and close as required.

PAINTED, COLLAGE OR DYED-FABRIC SCENERY

Background scenery may be painted on plywood, hardboard or a fabric such as unbleached calico.

A collage (material picture) can be effective, too. Use a large piece of fabric as the base, and glue or stitch material shapes on to it.

Fabric dyes are useful for creating a scene on white cotton sheeting. They may be painted or sponged on; either allow them to run into each other slightly, or pick out fine outlines with hot wax to keep the dyes apart. Batik is another process suitable for puppet theatre.

RELIEF SCULPTURED OR MODELLED SCENERY

Back-screens finished in relief can be very effective. Establish the shape in polystyrene on a plywood base, and cover it with paper and PVA glue, or

with stockinet and pearl glue. With stockinet, first soak it in hot water and then in carpenter's pearl glue; squeeze out the majority of the glue, and spread the fabric over the back-scene, pressing it carefully into the modelling. When dry, it will be quite stiff and strong.

Alternatively, use one of the modelling materials described in Chapter 3, building on to a lightweight base of balsa wood, polystyrene, cardboard boxes, or a frame of chicken-wire, as appropriate.

Fig 172 shows the effectiveness of sculptured arches with a plain back drape.

Fig 171 A painted backcloth for a scene from *Faustus* by Barry Smith's Theatre of Puppets

Fig 172 A scene from Keats' *Isabella (or the Pot of Basil)* by Barry Smith's Theatre of Puppets; skilful painting enhances the effect of sculptured arches, which are set against a plain black backcloth

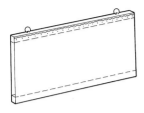

Fig 173 Attaching background scenery – (a) fixing to a batten and hanging by large screweyes;

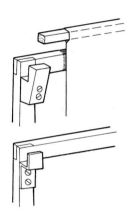

Fig 173 (b) wooden or metal brackets used to support a backcloth;

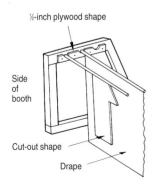

½-inch plywood shape

Side of booth

Cut-out shape

Drape

Fig 173 (c) a slotted batten for suspending backdrapes or cut-out scenery;

PROJECTED SCENERY

A translucent back-screen made from a rear-projection material or a suitable alternative, such as plain shower-curtain fabric, allows images to be projected from behind the booth. To use this approach for marionettes, the operators must work from a bridge, or they would obscure the path of the projected image. Arrange the stage lighting so that no strong light falls directly on to the screen. For more advice on projection techniques, *see* Chapter 8.

ATTACHING A HANGING BACKCLOTH

Either tack the top and bottom of the backcloth to two wooden battens, *or* slip the battens into wide hems. There are a variety of ways of attaching this to the main framework, as follows:

1. suspend the batten from hooks on the frame using large screw-eyes;

2. extend the top batten to fit into wooden or metal brackets screwed to the stage;

3. attach a slotted batten to the sides of the stage to hold a series of scenery battens or solid scenery sections in a proscenium booth for glove, hand and rod puppets.

ATTACHING A ROLL-UP BACKCLOTH

To raise and lower a fabric backcloth, tack the top to a batten and the bottom to a thick dowel. Roll up the scene around the dowel, then attach a strong cord to each end of this roller. Thread the cords over pulleys screwed into the batten. When the cords are released, the roller is lowered and the cords wind around each end of it. Pulling the cords causes them to unwind and the roller to roll up. The use of slotted brackets at each end of the back-frame permits a series of backcloths to be hung ready for various scenes.

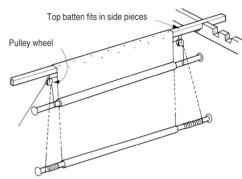

Top batten fits in side pieces

Pulley wheel

As the cord is raised, it unwinds, but winds up the scenery

As the roll unwinds, the cord winds round the dowel

Fig 173 (d) a roll-up backcloth;

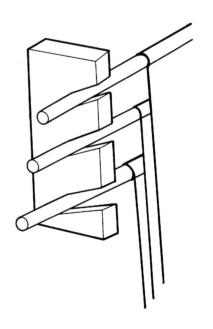

Fig 173 (e) slotted brackets to hold a series of backcloths

STAGING FOR SHADOW PUPPETS

Stage Construction

Both the table-top theatre and the flexible staging units (*see* pages 107-114), into which a frame with a screen attached is easily inserted, are suitable for shadow puppet staging. Other types of stage may also accommodate a shadow screen or combine shadows with other puppets.

Normally, the screen is attached to the audience side of the frame so that the lower cross-bar provides a ledge on which the puppets can walk. This will be satisfactory, provided the control is angled and not vertical.

The screen may have a ledge on which to rest the controls of characters which are 'in repose' on the screen, while the others are manipulated. Make the ledge from a strip of plywood, covered with thick felt, foam rubber, or a comparable material, so that the controls do not slide. Support the ledge with triangular wooden

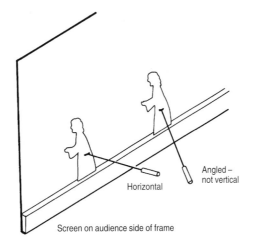

blocks hinged to the main frame; dowels glued into the ledge fit into holes drilled in the triangular blocks. Glue a narrow wooden batten to the edge of the ledge, to prevent controls slipping off.

When not in use, shadow puppets are normally placed on tables to the sides of the operating area, or on a table-top below the screen. Puppets with controls fixed horizontally are rested with the controls on the table, and the figures over the edge, to avoid

Fig 174 With the screen on the audience side of the frame, shadow puppets may be operated from directly behind or from below, at an angle to the screen

Screen on audience side of frame

Horizontal

Angled – not vertical

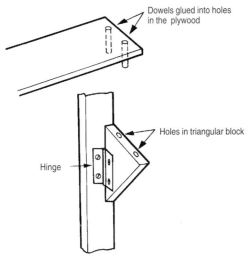

Dowels glued into holes in the plywood

Holes in triangular block

Hinge

Construction of the ledge

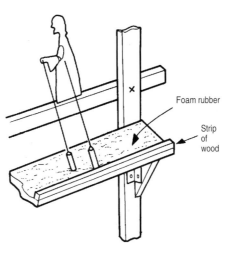

Foam rubber

Strip of wood

Holding the controls securely

Fig 175 Construction and use of a ledge for characters in repose

bending and other damage. Those with other types of control may be placed flat on the table.

The Screen

Make the screen from a reasonably strong, semi-opaque material. A piece of white cotton or polyester/cotton sheeting is satisfactory, but there are better methods – these include a lighting acetate known as 'frost', architects' tracing linen, or a plain white shower-curtain fabric. Rear-screen projection material is good but more expensive than the alternatives, which are quite adequate.

The screen must be taut, otherwise the performance will be marred. You may attach the screen to the frame with drawing pins (thumb-tacks), or staple it. A better solution with a fabric screen is to punch holes with eyelets around the edge, then thread thick cord through these and through large screw-eyes in the frame to hold it evenly taut. Then, if it sags, it is easily tightened.

Scenery

Beautiful scenes can be achieved by simple means. Often, a mere sugges-

tion will evoke an idea, and this can be more effective than elaborate scenery. Remember that puppets will be hidden by solid scenery, so every piece of scenery cuts down the acting area.

THE SHAPE OF THE SCREEN

The shape of the screen can help to set the scene; within the basic rectangle, a masking shape can be fastened against the screen to establish any other shape required. It may be a material drape, a cardboard cut-out, a thin sheet of ply-wood, or even a coloured sheet of translucent acetate.

Alternatively, the projection methods described in Chapter 8 allow any shape to be established, or even changed during a performance, without the need to carry large items of scenery. These also permit textured surfaces or lighting effects to be created across the entire screen.

CONSTRUCTING SCENERY

Solid black scenery is best made from stiff card or three-ply wood. For texture or colour, use one of the methods described for shadow puppets (*see* pages 97-101).

Scenery such as a door may be fixed with linen hinges glued on. Tape a

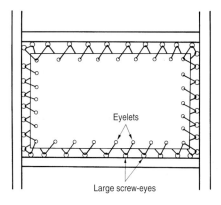

Fig 176 Keeping a shadow screen taut

Eyelets

Large screw-eyes

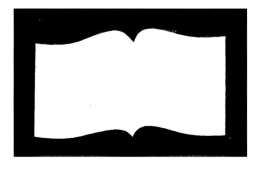

Fig 177 A masking shape for a shadow screen

Fig 178 Shadow scenery: strips of wood provide a walking surface for the puppets, and the door has a fabric hinge and a galvanized wire control

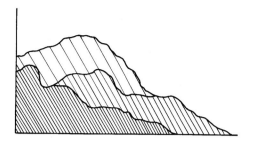

Fig 180 Multiple layers of tissue paper help to achieve a sense of depth

A horizon piece helps to create a feeling of greater depth in the scene. Most of the action takes place below this line, although smaller figures may be used above it for distant action. Multiple layers of tissue paper can also suggest depth; these are cut to required shapes and overlapped to produce a variety of intensities of colour or, with white, shades ranging from white to dark grey.

SECURING SCENERY TO THE SCREEN

Scenery may be held by drawing pins, paper clips, bulldog clips, hooks or button magnets, or by suspending it on a thread. Double-sided adhesive tape may be used, but it can show through the screen. The space between screen and framework makes a useful scenery slot. For a more substantial arrangement, attach a strip of wood to the lower cross-bar, with suitable plywood or aluminium spacers between them. Glue a stepped strip of aluminium or a block of wood and strip of plywood to the back of the scenery. The strip fits snugly into the slot and holds the scenery firmly against the screen. A similar arrangement at the top of the screen may be necessary for large items of scenery.

Fig 179 A horizon piece helps to create depth in a scene

small piece of galvanized wire to the moving part so that it can be opened and closed easily. If the puppet has to walk on the scenery, glue wooden blocks on to the back of the cut-out scene to provide a surface.

Fig 181 An aluminium or plywood strip attached to the back of scenery fits snugly into a scenery slot

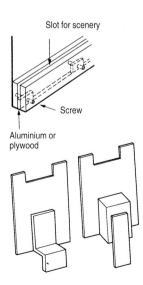

8 Lighting and Sound

LIGHTING THE PUPPET THEATRE

Artificial lighting should create atmosphere, enhance modelling and focus the audience's attention; it should not obscure visibility. The size of most puppets creates problems of visibility and their proximity to the back-drop in many stages can make it difficult to distinguish them from the scenery. As a basic principle, therefore, the puppets should be lit separately from the sets whenever possible.

In a fairly large fit-up, backcloth lighting can be positioned behind wing flats; however, this is more problematic in a small stage, and you will need to consider this when designing the stage. When separate lighting is not possible because of staging limitations or economics, choose colour filters that will enhance the puppets and subdue the sets. Additionally, avoid very dimly lit scenes; puppets often require more light than human theatre for a comparable scene.

Generally, more lights of lower power give greater flexibility and more subtle lighting than a few high-powered lamps. This is helpful if you have little space; a number of more modest lights should be adequate for a small stage and require far less space than one or two professional lanterns. Open staging makes various lighting schemes possible, but the larger the performance area,

Fig 182 The Little Angel Theatre production of *Sleeping Beauty*. As the puppets ascend the tower in the lift, the puppeteers follow them up the tower and operate them in view of the audience. The lighting of the set is accomplished with great care

the more lanterns you will need to light it effectively.

Lighting to the top of puppets' heads casts heavy shadows on their faces, while horizontal or near-horizontal lighting flattens modelling, and produces large shadows on sets. When lighting the acting area, try to angle lights within a range of about 30-60 degrees.

To eliminate unwanted shadows, try to reduce or re-direct light; compensating with another light is not very satisfactory, as it brightens scenery, throwing the puppets into silhouette. Otherwise, light the acting area with a lantern with a soft-edged beam, as these are less noticeable than hard edges; try also to direct the light so that its edges fall upon an architectural edge in the scenery, such as a door frame, a pillar or picture frame. A prism convex lantern or a fresnel will serve this purpose for on-stage side-lighting, with a variable focus profile spotlight for front-of-house use. Remember also to consider the dramatic potential of shadow.

For back-stage lighting, use blue low-power bulbs, heavily shaded so that light does not spill on to the stage area. Make sure that huge shadows of the puppeteers operating back-stage are not being cast on surrounding walls and ceilings.

When attaching lighting to the outside of a fit-up, ensure that it is suitably positioned or shielded, so that it does not dazzle or distract the audience.

Different Types of Lighting

Apart from lights for special effects and backcloth or cyclorama illumination, lighting may be categorized into sidelights, front-of-house lights, overhead lights, and footlights.

SIDELIGHTS

Sidelights provide much of the illumination for puppet presentations, and enhance the modelling of the puppets. A mixture of floodlights and spotlights is possible, with spotlights used mainly for brighter effects. PAR 38 floods and spots are often used and, from the professional range, prism (or pebble) convex spotlights and fresnels are versatile and compact. Fresnels can be adjusted to provide anything from a soft-edged spot to a medium-angle flood. Some requirements call for profile spotlights, which are normally positioned outside the fit-up because of their size and power.

Within a fit-up, sidelights may be placed to each side of a proscenium opening and behind wing flats. Sidelights may also be placed well clear of the stage in the auditorium; this is more common practice with open-stage techniques, but may also be appropriate with proscenium stages if the light is directed carefully through the opening.

The number of lights needed will depend on the size of the stage. As a guide, a fit-up about 3m wide by 2m deep (10 × 6ft) might have on each side two fresnels or small floodlights for the down-stage (front) acting area, two for the mid-stage area, and one or two floodlights for backcloth illumination. When lighting a small open stage, two spotlights or fresnels are the minimum necessary to highlight modelling and eliminate heavy shadows; adding just two lights will increase the scope considerably.

FRONT-OF-HOUSE SPOTLIGHTS

These spotlights are placed in the auditorium. While on-stage sidelights enhance modelling, front lighting improves visibility, so the task is to find an appropriate balance between the two. Fresnel spots as front-of-house sidelights are very helpful, and one major profile spotlight (500-650 watt) from behind the audience is usually satisfactory. With proscenium theatres, the precision of profile spotlights might be needed rather than fresnels.

OVERHEAD LIGHTING

Overhead lighting is not often used, due to various considerations: space, the logistics of fixing, problems caused by lighting the top of puppets' heads, and the fact that it may produce a wash of light over too large an area. When it is used, it is generally floodlighting placed over a proscenium arch, or suspended above, and just in front of, an open booth.

FOOTLIGHTS

Footlights (floodlighting along the front of the stage floor) are seldom used today. Their main purpose is usually to balance overhead lighting, which is comparatively little used in puppet theatre. They can obscure the figures, and are often too powerful and too close to the puppets, causing lighting flare on costumes and faces; they may also produce 'rising' shadows that vary in height as the puppets move up- and down-stage. When a little footlighting is needed, most floodlights are too large, so use ordinary striplights in a suitable lighting box designed to carry coloured filters.

BACKCLOTH ILLUMINATION

The illumination of the backcloth may be achieved in puppet theatre by floodlights mounted in the wings, by an 'electrics groundrow' (floor-level uplighting), or by overhead illumination, depending on the staging. In smaller stages, striplights may be used. Fresnels that adjust to a medium-angle flood might be found useful too. The general rule is to try to avoid lights which have a hard-edged beam. (*See also* the section on projectors, page 145, for details of rear-projection effects.)

Lighting for Glove and Rod Puppets

In principle, these puppets need side- and back-lighting from the wings to illuminate puppets and sets. Overhead floodlights can be useful, but footlights are not recommended. Front-of-house profile spotlights are helpful, but can emphasize the small size of the puppets. Illumination of a cyclorama or sky-cloth helps to create depth. The following advice shows how this is often translated into practice.

OPEN BOOTHS

You can light a small booth with reflector floodlights, spotlights, or sealed-beam (PAR) reflector spotlights mounted on wooden extension arms attached to the front corners of the stage. Often there is little space in the booth, but clip-on domestic fitments with floodlights or spotlights may be introduced to highlight the backcloth or sets.

For larger booths, fresnels and other spotlights mounted on telescopic stands just in front and to either side of the stage are efficient. You may introduce lighting from the wings and below the backcloth, but ensure that shadows of the puppeteers are not cast on the sets. A front-of-house profile spotlight mounted on a stand is often helpful. If conditions permit, overhead floodlighting may be used, but a travelling show will seldom find a suitable means of securing it.

PROSCENIUM BOOTHS

It is difficult to illuminate a small proscenium booth with lighting in the auditorium, and lighting within the booth itself may be too close to the puppets. The most satisfactory solution is to mount small spotlights to the top corners of the booth, outside the proscenium arch, and carefully directed on to the acting area. Try to achieve adequate illumination of both the playboard and the mid-stage areas. Backcloth illumination is achieved with striplights.

With a larger proscenium booth, wherever possible, mount the main lighting inside the booth in keeping with the principles outlined above. Overhead floodlights may be secured inside the proscenium or from a batten supported in front of the backcloth. Some lighting may be placed outside the booth – a front-of-house profile spotlight and sidelights will be fine, if they are carefully directed through the proscenium arch.

Some stages are designed with a projection like a curtain pelmet outside the booth, above the proscenium arch; this houses small fresnels or spotlights, and allows light to be shone into the booth very precisely. Floodlights tend not to be used outside a booth, as their light will spill on to the curtains.

Lighting for Marionettes

In stages with no bridge, the puppets can be operated at no more than arm's length from the backcloth, so it is difficult to light puppets and sets separately, unless lights can be positioned behind wing flats without impeding puppet entrances and exits. When there is a bridge, it is possible to place lighting under the bridge floor, or in a well below stage level, to light the back-screen and increase the sense of depth on the stage. When backcloths cannot be illuminated separately, it helps if they are not too light in colour, to enhance the visibility of puppets, and reduce the effect of unwanted shadows.

OPEN STAGES

For small stages, two lights – one to each side of the stage and cross-lighting the acting area – are the minimum requirement. However, at least two lights to each side are recommended, preferably prism convex spots or fresnels. For larger stages, more side-lighting may be needed, possibly supplemented by floodlights, although fresnels will often provide a useful compromise. A front-of-house profile spotlight is desirable.

PROSCENIUM STAGES

These stages utilize sidelights, overhead lights (if conditions permit), at least one front-of-house profile spotlight and, occasionally, a groundrow for illuminating the backcloth. Front-of-house lights to the sides of the auditorium illuminate the apron of the stage, which would otherwise be in shadow. Overhead lighting may be attached to the inside of the proscenium, or under the floor of a bridge.

Lighting for Shadow Puppets

In principle, it is possible to use any source of light for shadow play, but it is normal to use only one source at a time, as two lights produce a blurred shadow. Some professional performers use a selection of lights and projectors, fading from one to another for specific purposes. Although 'live' light is the traditional method, and the flickering light gives added movement to the figures, safety considerations make it unacceptable for most purposes.

It is possible to operate from behind, as well as below, the screen only when using daylight, a reading lamp, or a fluorescent striplight (*see* below). Powerful light sources require you to operate from below, but also allow you to increase the size of the shadow by moving the puppet towards the light. With other lights, the image will tend to fade when you do this.

DAYLIGHT

Ordinary daylight is sufficient for home or classroom use. Position the screen between a window and the audience; only the shadows of the puppets held against the screen will show, not the performers. Bright sunlight gives a stronger shadow, but shadows of window frames and performers might appear too.

READING LAMP WITH SPOTLIGHT

A floor-standing or table-top lamp with a heavy base may provide an adequate light. It must be positioned so that the performers can operate without casting their shadows on the screen, and without knocking it over. In practice, this means it is usually placed just to one side of the screen.

FLUORESCENT STRIPLIGHT

A fluorescent tube and fitment may be mounted behind the screen, either attached to the framework above the screen, or on a suitable base for stability below the screen. It provides a good diffused light, casts no shadows of performers nor control rods, and remains cool. Colour effects are also possible.

PROFESSIONAL SPOTLIGHT OR FLOODLIGHT

One of these lights, mounted on a telescopic stand, provides a good, crisp, clear source. Take care with positioning, or the source of light will be very obvious and distracting to the audience.

PROJECTORS

A projector gives a strong, crisp light and allows the projection of scenery to fill a large screen. A purpose-built lighting unit with a quartz iodine bulb (*see* page 146) is excellent for large-scale work. An overhead projector also offers possibilities for creating a variety of images (*see* page 145). A slide projector provides a satisfactory light, but imposes more constraints than the two other methods.

Lighting Control

For most puppet presentations, the lights are carefully directed before the performance and remain in the same position throughout. Therefore, in terms of lighting control, the puppeteer is concerned simply with 'raising' and 'dimming' different lights in order to achieve the required effects. Being able to adjust the lighting assists not only in the creation of atmosphere, but also allows a variation in the intensity of the lighting from each side, highlighting modelling and avoiding flatness in faces.

Because of the scale of puppet theatre, and the proximity of the lighting to the puppets, each light should ideally have its own dimmer control. For economy, lights may be paired or grouped, if the desired effect can be achieved this way, and provided that the maximum load specified for each channel is not exceeded.

If you are using a microphone, make sure that the dimmers will not interfere with the sound system; some units might cause a slight hum.

Colour Lighting

Coloured lighting can create or enhance atmosphere but, used carelessly, can also detract from a performance. Any light may be coloured by covering its source with a colour filter. Professional lighting acetates are available in a wide range of colours and are of different types as certain lamps require high-temperature filters. They may be purchased in sheets or pre-cut sizes, then mounted in metal frames supplied with the lights. Manufacturers produce sample books of colour filters.

Avoid too much strong colour, as this reduces visibility. Remember, filters do not *add* colour; they work by filtering out other colours of the spectrum. This can be limiting because an object responds sympathetically to coloured lighting only if that object contains pigment of the same basic colour as the light. A deep blue takes out all but the blue part of the spectrum, but a pale blue tint lets through all the blue but also a proportion of the other colours, so there is always some response from the object lit. Therefore, pale tints are generally more useful than deep colours.

To create atmosphere without reducing visibility, try using somewhat deeper colours for backcloth lighting and some side-lighting, but use neutrals and pale tints for lighting the fronts of the puppets, to ensure visibility.

The use of slightly different colours from each side helps to enhance modelling of faces, but note that varying the intensity of the light creates a variation in colour and, conversely, changes in colour affect the intensity of a light. Therefore, avoid overdoing the contrast between the two sides by too great a difference in both colour and intensity. Note also that even cool colours become warmer as a light is dimmed, because the filament becomes redder.

There is an important difference between mixing (overlaying) filters and mixing coloured lights. Because filters take out parts of the colour spectrum, the use of two filters together on one light reduces further the emerging colour. On the other hand, overlaying colours from different lights actually builds up the light by adding parts of the spectrum.

John Wright, who created beautiful pictures with his lighting effects at the Little Angel Theatre, suggested starting colour explorations with eight lights for a proscenium booth:

	Stage left	Stage right	Position and direction
Fresnel spots	Steel blue	Light amber	Outside proscenium directed to front of acting area
Floodlights	Turquoise blue	Medium blue	Inside proscenium directed to front of acting area
Floodlights	Magenta red	Steel blue	Inside proscenium directed to mid-stage area
Floodlights	Medium blue	Light turquoise blue	Behind wing flats directed to backcloth

Wright recommended setting up the puppets on-stage and switching on all the lights, then dimming each one separately to see the effect of each combination of lights. This is excellent advice and a good basis on which to add further lights. Bear in mind that these were modest-power floodlights on a stage of a reasonable size. In some circumstances you might try replacing floodlights with small spotlights or fresnels for the illumination of the acting areas.

Where a substantial number of lights is used, changing colour involves dimming one set and raising another. In a stage with only a few lights, select the colours carefully, because exchanging hot filters between scenes is not recommended and often not possible because of their situation. Units with remote control permit smooth colour changes, but they are expensive, require a good deal of space, and reduce the flexibility and subtlety offered by more lights, which can be blended to create various effects.

Organizing the Lighting

Organizing the lighting in a small stage with a few lights may mean simply redirecting existing lights and trying different colour filters and dimmer positions. With ambitious productions, a more systematic approach becomes necessary.

First, determine what you would like to achieve and design scenery with a view to your lighting needs and where you will put the lights. Lights with a fixed position provide a starting point around which you can arrange other lights.

Next, determine a colour filter for each light, although this might be modified later.

Now prepare a full plan. Show which lamps are linked to the same circuit and number each lamp with its switchboard channel; show its position, arrow the direction in which it points, and note where it is focused. As the performance takes shape, update the plan.

With the lights fixed in position, insert the colour filters and adjust the focus as appropriate. During rehearsals, with the puppets under the lights, clarify lighting needs, and prepare a list of cues ('the cue sheet'). Number each cue on the script and on the cue sheet, note the page, the cue number, the timing of the change (whether to take 30 seconds, snap on or off, and so on), and a description of the effect. Modify the plan as necessary, and prepare a 'switchboard plot' showing the cue number, the timing, and the action to be taken (in other words, the number of the light and its switchboard position – full on, half, three-quarters, or as a percentage).

Ensure that lamps are not near any flammable materials, and leads will not impede or trip performers. Leads to front-of-house lights must be carefully routed, and securely taped down if across the floor; lighting stands must be sturdy, secure and positioned so that they do not present a danger to the audience.

With the show in performance some adjustments might be necessary, but the main task is regular checking of the equipment. Are all the bulbs in good order? Are the reflectors and lenses clean? Are the wiring and plugs in good order and all connections secure? Do any fuses need replacing? Are there sufficient spare fuses and bulbs?

Finally, remember that lighting control needs to be undertaken with as much care as puppet manipulation. Paying attention to the basics, like the

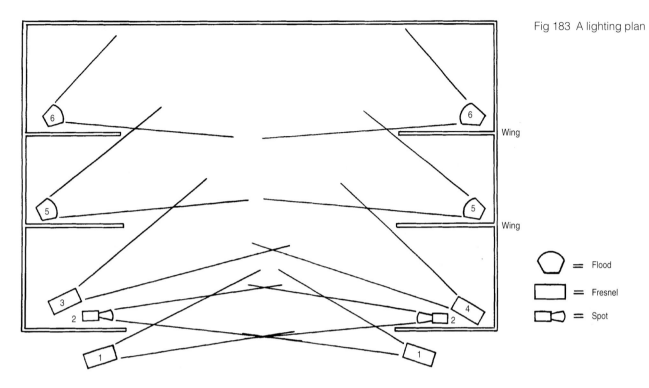

Fig 183 A lighting plan

Wing

Wing

= Flood

= Fresnel

= Spot

Fig 184 A lighting cue sheet

LIGHTING CUES: ACT TWO

SCRIPT PAGE	CUE	TIMING	EFFECT
22	OPENING	PRESET	GLOWING GATES OF HELL
23	1	15 SECS.	GATES OPEN SLOWLY ILLUMINATING CENTRE STAGE
25	2	SNAP	DEVIL APPEARS - HIGHLIGHT
27	3	10 SECS.	THUNDER AND LIGHTNING
28	4	20 SECS.	SCENE TRANSFORMS TO SEASHORE

Fig 185 A switchboard plot

SWITCHBOARD PLOT: ACT THREE

CUE	TIMING	ACTION
OPENING	PRESET	$\frac{1 \quad 2}{50\%}$ $\frac{3}{70\%}$ $\frac{4}{60\%}$ $\frac{5 \quad 6}{10\%}$
1	SNAP	$\frac{1 \quad 2 \quad 3 \quad 4}{30\%}$ $\frac{5 \quad 6}{70\%}$
2	15 SECS.	$\frac{1}{50\%}$ $\frac{2}{60\%}$ $\frac{3 \quad 4 \quad 5 \quad 6}{40\%}$
3	10 SECS.	$\frac{1}{75\%}$ $\frac{3 \quad 4}{60\%}$ $\frac{5}{50\%}$ $\frac{6}{80\%}$

way the house-lights go down (slowly and quietly, not suddenly plunging the audience into darkness) is very important if you want to avoid destroying the atmosphere.

Lighting Equipment

The lighting equipment most useful for puppeteers is described below. There is a lighting scheme to suit every budget. Professional lighting hire for a day or two is reasonably priced, and this will allow you try out lamps before buying.

Each of the professional lights described has a tilting fork, which allows the lantern to be adjusted to

many positions. There is also a variety of mounting devices to attach the lamps to a ceiling, wall, metal pipe, telescopic stand, or part of the stage.

SPOTLIGHTS

Reflector spotlight and PAR spotlight (up to 150 watt) Reflector spotlights are held in display or domestic lighting fitments. Most common is the sealed-beam reflector spotlight known as a PAR 38 (Parabolic Aluminised Reflector), which is available in a small range of colours, and clear. It provides good lighting for small stages. Clear lights may need improvised holders for colour filters.

There is also a PAR 16 lantern which uses 20-75 watt lamps. It comes complete with a casing (15cm long by 5cm in diameter/6 × 2in), which takes colour frames and a 'barn-door' attachment for shaping the beam. Attach the lantern to a non-combustible surface.

Small but quite powerful units designed for domestic use, such as quartz halogen spotlights, can be useful, but you must ensure that the light produced is adequate and does not create any unwanted patterning of light.

Fresnel spotlight (250-650 watt) This is generally the smallest, lightest and most versatile professional light, good for side-lighting within a fit-up as its light is easier to blend on the stage than that of other spotlights. Fresnels have a soft-edged circular beam, the spread of which may be varied from a near-parallel beam to a medium-angle flood (about 10-40 degrees or 20-60 degrees). Barn-door attachments shape the beam, but you need to check that the lantern you choose can be used with barn-doors and colour filters simultaneously.

Fig 186 A selection of modest-powered lighting units:

① – a domestic reflector spotlight with a 40 watt bulb;

② and ③ – purpose-built aluminium light-boxes for mounting on the stage or on telescopic stands (2 has a 100 watt reflector spotlight, 3 has a 100 watt reflector floodlight and colour filters);

④ – a domestic 150 watt PAR38 clear spotlight in a wall-mounting fitment;

⑤ – a domestic PAR 38 fitment with a 150 watt coloured floodlight. The fitment has been adapted to fit on to aluminium tubing. The tubing attaches to a bracket which bolts on to the side of an open stage;

⑥ – a 60 watt striplight and holder mounted in a purpose-built aluminium fitment with a bracket that bolts on to the stage

Prism convex (or pebble convex) spotlight (250 watt-650 watt) This is a useful compromise between a fresnel and a profile spotlight. It avoids the problems of filament projection with some profiles at close range, and flare around the beam's edge with a fresnel (which is about the same price). The angle of the beam is usually variable, from about 10 degrees to 60 degrees, making this a flexible, compact lamp. Again, make sure your chosen model can be used with colour filters and a barn-door attachment simultaneously.

Profile spotlight (250-650 watt) This is excellent for open-stage performance, for a front-of-house spotlight with proscenium theatres, and for shadow play. It may be used also for side-lighting within very large theatres, provided that the lamp is not too powerful.

It produces a variable circular beam, which, on different models, may be adjusted from approximately 15-25 degrees or 20-40 degrees. Built-in shutters permit the beam to be shaped and the edges of the beam can usually be sharpened or softened. The throw of this sort of light would typically be around 9m (30ft), although long-throw (15m/50ft) versions are available. Profile spotlights tend to be longer, heavier and less flexible for use inside a puppet stage than the other lanterns described, and are around fifty per cent more expensive than a fresnel or prism convex spotlight.

Follow spots (c. 650 watt) These lamps, which project a spot of about 6-16 degrees to follow a character on stage, are normally too heavy, too powerful, too expensive and unnecessary for puppet theatre. However, more modest versions are available if the facility is required.

FLOODLIGHTS

Reflector floodlight and PAR 38 floodlight (up to 150 watt) Floodlights used for domestic or display lighting are compact and ideal for use in restricted spaces. Unless you use coloured lamps, you may have to improvise a fitment for holding colour filters, as a wash of clear light will be of little use. Their use for open-stage performances is limited as they may give too great a spread of light, but they may be used for floodlighting within a fit-up and for shadow play.

Mini-floodlight (100-250 watt) Most floodlights are too bulky and illuminate too large an area for puppet theatre, but mini-floodlights are much more suitable in terms of size, weight and power. This professional floodlight has a wide-angle, evenly distributed beam, and can be used with or without colour filters and barn-doors to limit the spread of light. These are useful within larger proscenium stages and generally need to be at least 1.5m (5ft) away from the area they illuminate. Separate lights, which can be directed individually, are preferable to three- or four-compartment floodlights.

STRIPLIGHTS

Non-fluorescent striplights (60–70 watt) These tubular domestic lights may be useful for the illumination of a sky-cloth in a small stage, and for special effects. Those with a pearl/opaque finish are best, as clear lights can have some filament projection. The fitments may be attached to part of the stage, a well in the stage floor, or held in a home-made, suitably ventilated, light box, which may need to be grooved or have runners for colour filters. Fluorescent tubes are not suitable for this type of use.

Fig 187 A range of professional lanterns by Strand Lighting, of a size and power useful for puppet theatre – (a) the Quartet F Mk2 Fresnel Spotlight;

Fig 187 (b) the Quartet PC MK2 Prism-Convex Spotlight;

Fig 187 (c) the Quartet Profile Spotlight;

Fig 187 (d) the Miniflood Mk2

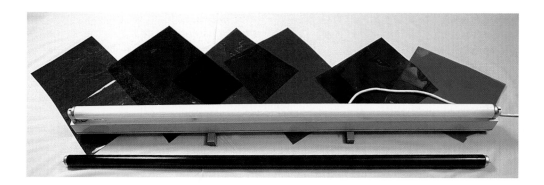

Fig 188 A fluorescent striplight in a domestic fitment and with colour filters.

Also shown is an ultra-violet striplight, which fits into the same domestic fitment

Fluorescent striplights (c. 36-70 watt)
Fluorescent lighting, available in various lengths, is not appropriate for normal stage use but provides adequate light for shadow play. Tubes and fitments are modestly priced but take care to protect the light during transportation. As the tube remains quite cool, colour effects may be achieved simply by placing colour filters over it, but it is best to construct a light box to contain the tube, with runners to carry the filters. Ensure that the tube is completely covered by the filters, otherwise intrusive, clear, diffused light will destroy much of the colour.

PROJECTORS

A projector can provide excellent lighting for shadow play and for the rear-projection of scenery and other images for all types of puppet. It influences stage design, since sufficient clear space between the projector and the screen is required, and the projector must be square to the screen to prevent any distortion of the image.

Overhead projectors These units give a crisp light for shadow play or projected scenery. Transparencies can be coloured with suitable felt pens, glass-painting colours or shapes cut from transparent, self-adhesive film. For silhouette effects, textured materials and cardboard cut-outs may be used, or you can paint on to acetate with quick-drying black enamel. Coloured acetate sheets can be used to cover the entire area and non-naturalistic images can be achieved by standing patterned, translucent objects on the projector and by varying the focus. With ingenuity a variety of effects can be achieved. To keep transparencies flat on the projector, mount them in cardboard frames. Some portable projectors create no noise, as they need no built-in cooling fan.

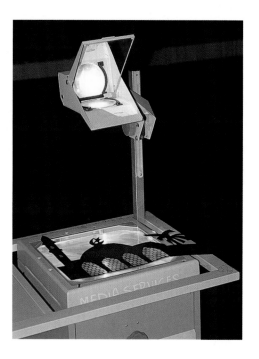

Fig 189 An overhead projector used to illuminate shadow play and to project scenery, either for shadow play or for three-dimensional puppets

Slide projectors Slide projectors hold a large number of slides and require the minimum of attention during a performance, but they can have noisy cooling fans and need a substantial distance to cast a large image. A wide-angle lens helps to reduce this distance. You can project photographic slides of real scenes or your own designs. Scenery and other images can be projected in silhouette or full colour. To avoid the audience seeing a slide change, or to facilitate the superimposition of images, use two projectors linked to a dimmer desk with a cross-fade facility. It is then possible to dissolve from one scene to the next and move each projector on to the next slide or scene while it is not projecting.

A purpose-built projection unit A suitably qualified person can construct a lighting unit that provides a consider-able spread of light (up to 4m/13ft wide) at a comparatively short distance from the screen. The light can be used for shadow play or to project images on to a shadow screen, or a back-screen for other puppets. The cost is only a fraction of that of the other projection units described.

The unit consists of a quartz iodine bulb (24 volt/50 watt) mounted in an aluminium, ventilated light box, and connected to the mains via a transformer. The inside of the box is painted with heat-resistant matt-black paint, to prevent reflection. It is mounted on one end of a wooden bar. On the other end of the bar is fastened a scenery frame.

The scenery frame is a rectangular wooden frame with grooves to take cut-out cardboard silhouette scenes or home-made transparencies of scenery. It should have at least two grooves, so that one scene can be inserted as

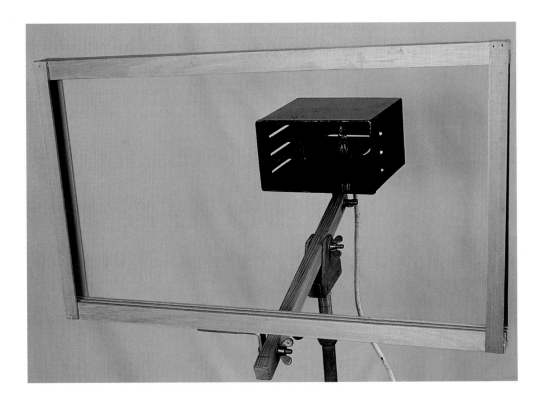

Fig 190 (a) A purpose-built projection unit mounted on a telescopic stand;

another is removed, or images can be superimposed. A masking card, giving a particular shape to the screen, can also be retained in one runner while scenery within the shape can be changed in the other; alternatively, large colour filters can be used in one runner, with scenery in the other.

The light box and scenery frame each need a bracket, which bolts on to the central bar and allows adjustment as necessary. The central wooden bar is mounted on a telescopic stand. When determining where to position the box and frame on the central bar, ensure that no light spills over the outside of the frame. Arrange the dimensions so that the edges of the beam fall on to the frame itself.

Scenery for projection can be made as described for overhead projectors (*see* page 145). When cutting out silhouettes from cardboard, leave the edge of the sheet as a frame. Other items of scenery can be taped to the front of the frame if required – dry grasses, and many other objects, have been used to good effect.

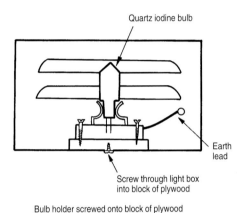

Fig 190 (b) mounting the bulb;

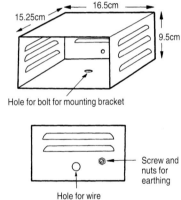

Fig 190 (c) the light-box;

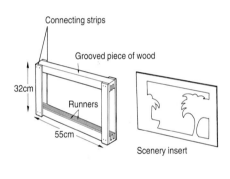

Fig 190 (d) the scenery frame;

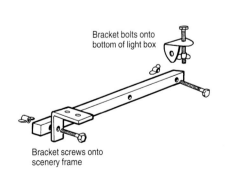

Fig 190 (e) the central bar;

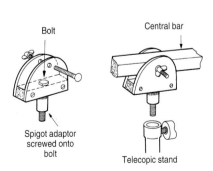

Fig 190 (f) the 'U' bracket;

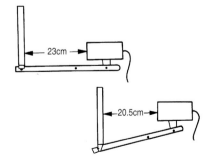

Fig 190 (g) the distance between the light-box and the frame alters as the central bar is angled to permit the light to shine through the centre of the frame

Fig 191 A scene from *Peer Gynt* by the Little Angel Theatre, using coloured projected images with black-shadow figures

professional stage-lighting stands. These stands are sturdy, strong and capable of holding more than one of the professional lights described. Typical height adjustments for different models are approximately 1-1.5m (3-5ft), 1.2-2.25m (4-7½ft), or 1.5-3.3m (5-11ft). A 'spigot adaptor' screws over the lamp's suspension bolt and fits into the top of the stand. Some types of stand are also useful for supporting items of scenery, but they must be placed out of the way of the operators.

LIGHTING CONTROL

Domestic lighting controls Small, lightweight dimmers with up to four control knobs, which are intended for domestic use, may be sufficient for small stages.

ULTRA-VIOLET LIGHTING

Ultra-violet tubes use the same fitments as domestic fluorescent striplights and, apart from colour, are the same in appearance. They illuminate objects covered or painted with UV materials up to a distance of about 2.4m (8ft) in 'black light' techniques (*see* page 150). They may be connected direct to the mains electricity supply.

TELESCOPIC STANDS FOR LIGHTS

Except in a permanent theatre with architectural points for fixtures, lights outside a booth are mounted on adjustable telescopic stands. Lightweight photographic stands are always in danger of being knocked over, so use

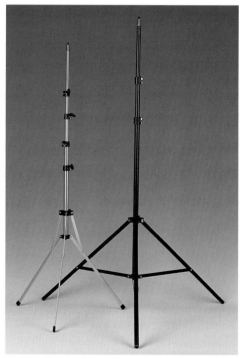

Fig 192 Telescopic lighting stands by Strand Lighting

Most units handle a maximum of 250 to 400 watts per control channel. Some units have three or four individual control knobs, with one master-control that overrides them all, but these are not easy to find. Domestic dimmers with a capacity of up to 650 watts have become available recently for use with individual lights; these may be useful for some puppet theatres.

Medium-range control units The problems with most professional lighting control units are the size, the weight and the price, but there are a few small lightweight units with integral controls and dimmer packs. These are somewhat limited in capacity but reasonably versatile; increases in capacity and versatility are matched by increases in price.

Larger lighting control systems These systems generally have large, heavy dimmer packs, which are accommodated out of the way, while a lightweight control desk, linked to the packs by long cables, can be situated wherever it is needed. The possibilities range from fairly basic but versatile systems with a few channels, to highly complex computerized schemes and remote radio control. However, as technology develops, systems that are currently too large and expensive for puppet theatres will inevitably appear in more appropriate forms.

Lights with dimmers attached Another recent development is professional lighting to which may be attached small individual dimmer units, controlled from a master desk. As yet, the

Fig 193 A range of lighting and control equipment by Zero 88 Lighting:

(top centre) a lantern from the Focus 650 range, suitable for many puppet theatre applications, accepting 300, 500, or 650 watt lamps;

(right) Alphapack, a 3-channel portable dimmer pack with three faders and a capacity of 6.3 amps per channel. It can be wall- or stand-mounted and controlled either directly on the pack itself or by a remote unit;

(top left) Level 6, a six-channel, single preset desk with a master fader, the most modest in a range of control desks used in conjunction with separate dimmer packs;

(bottom left) Level 12, a twelve-channel, two preset control desk, the next step up from the Level 6; Level 18 and 24 versions are also available

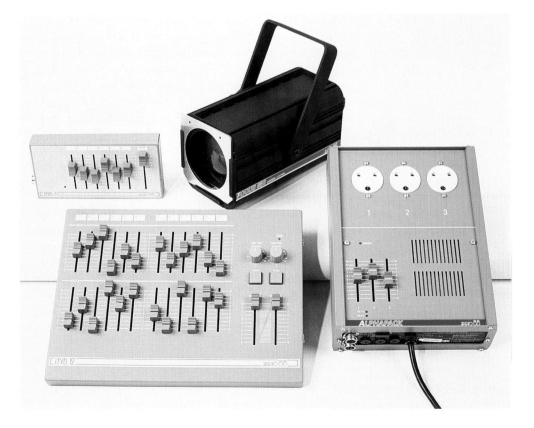

Fig 194 Lighting control by Strand Lighting:

Fig 194 (a) Act 6+ dimmer packs, which may be stored in a convenient position. Each pack has six 10-amp dimmers;

Fig 194 (b) Act 6D, a six-channel, single preset control board for the Act 6+ dimmer packs. It may be mounted on or off the stage or hand-held

lights tend to be rather large and expensive for puppet theatre, but the arrangement has obvious attractions and the technology exists; look out for appropriate developments.

BLACK LIGHT TECHNIQUE

The term 'black light theatre' or 'black theatre' in the puppetry context refers to a form of presentation that is used either for a whole production or sometimes only for special effects. It involves holding puppets in carefully directed beams of light (a curtain of light across the stage, illuminated from the sides), or using ultra-violet lighting with the puppets painted and dressed with fluorescent materials. Companies specializing in black light theatre may use both techniques together in the same production.

The rest of the stage, which has a black background and floor covering, remains completely dark. The operators dress in loose, jet-black clothes (made from dress velvet) with plenty of overlap, velvet hoods with black gauze sight panels, and long, black cotton gloves, making them invisible to the audience. Puppeteers who normally

require spectacles for performing need to wear contact lenses, as spectacles reflect the light.

One of the advantages of black light is the way in which the performers are released from the confines of a booth and able to utilize a larger area, without being visible. However, some performers prefer to work within a large booth, as the darkness then seems more intense and the effect is enhanced. The performers have to be careful not to let their bodies or limbs get in front of the puppets or the beams of light as they move about the stage, so their choreography is very important.

Black light makes a variety of effects possible, facilitated by extra invisible pairs of hands; black-backed objects can appear or disappear just by being turned; black shapes cut out as stencils allow background colours to show through, and objects can be mounted on black boards without the mount showing. Scenery created on a black velvet base and rolled up can suddenly appear as if by magic, just by unfurling the roll. Tricks and transformations are easily arranged and a colourful world of fantasy can be brought to life.

More complicated effects can also be achieved. For example, a figure or

Fig 195 (a) Black light technique, using ultra-violet lighting, for a production of *Aladdin* by the International Purves Puppets;

piece of scenery may be painted with an ordinary (not dark) paint, and then painted over with invisible, transparent, fluorescent colours. By changing from ordinary lighting to ultra-violet lighting, the paint underneath 'disappears' and the fluorescent paint glows, and vice versa. It is essential to test both the ordinary and fluorescent paints under both types of lighting to ensure that each produces the desired effect.

Several technical points are worth noting. If you are using 'clear white' rather than UV lighting, you will need a bank of three or four spotlights to each side of the stage, carefully shaped and sharply focused to produce horizontal beams of light across the stage. Profile spotlights are best; fresnels create beams with too soft an edge. Keep the lights as close as possible to the acting area, to prevent the beams spreading too widely. Occasionally, a little

colour lighting is introduced, but check that this does not change the colour, and therefore the invisibility, of the puppeteers' costumes. The lights must be suitably masked from the audience, usually behind black-covered flats.

For UV effects, Ian Purves (of Purves Puppets, an international company specializing in UV) recommends three fluorescent tubes for stages up to 6m (20ft) wide, one along the front of the stage floor, and one vertically to each side of the stage behind the proscenium or wing flats, as close to the front as possible. Wider stages would require an additional tube along the stage floor, but too much UV lighting will reveal the performers. The lights must be kept low, to illuminate the puppets and not the puppeteers. If the performers operate near the 2.4m (8ft) range of the lights, the puppets can be held within range while they themselves keep

Fig 195 (b) *Nessie the Loch Ness Monster*, a UV production by the International Purves Puppets, the Biggar Little Theatre, Biggar, Scotland

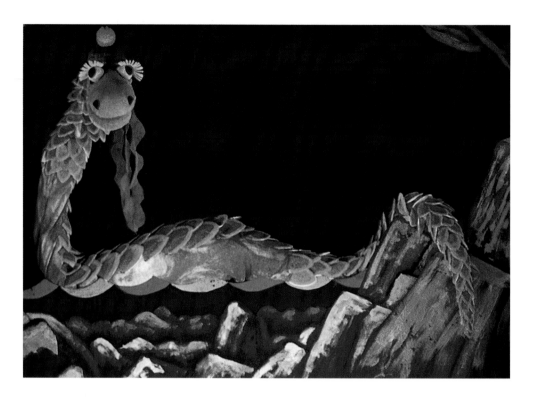

beyond it, thus reducing their visibility. This arrangement works effectively with puppets up to 120cm (4ft) tall.

Ultra-violet rays are invisible and harmless, but they cause certain materials to emit cold light, or to 'fluoresce'. This is most effective when the room or hall is totally blacked out; large, black, plastic bags and masking tape provide a solution where a little light remains.

There are different kinds of fluorescent colours. Some are visible only under black light and invisible under any other type of lighting; others are visible under all kinds of lighting, but much stronger under ultra-violet lights. To produce a stronger glow, it is best to have a light-coloured base upon which to paint the fluorescent colours. The colours can be mixed, but this does not produce the same colours as ordinary paints; for example, blue and yellow do not give green, but an off-white glow. Experiment with fluores-

cent colours under ultra-violet lighting, but see how they look under ordinary lighting too.

Ultra-violet materials and others with similar fluorescent properties are widely available, including felt pens with fluorescent colours, 'Dayglo' papers and self-adhesive labels, and paints that are applied with a brush or using a spray-can. Actual ultra-violet fabrics are not so common; they are obtainable from theatrical fabric specialists, but the range of colours is quite limited and some of these are not as effective as you might wish. However, experimenting is the answer for fabrics; you will find a range of soft fabrics and nets that meets your needs. Explore the off-cuts of friends' dressmaking activities and collect small samples from shops to test at home.

Other products that will glow under ultra-violet lighting include corn starch, mentholatum and petroleum jelly; washing powders that contain a 'blue' ingredient may be used on fabric, but take care not to rinse it out. These materials transmit a bluish-white light and may be used for some effects if fluorescent paint is not available.

Puppeteers who have to perform very close to their audience, as in some cabaret shows, sometimes employ 'pygmy' 15-watt lights as 'blinders'. These are placed around the stage area at about 30cm (12in) intervals, facing the audience and shielded from the operators. They appear decorative, but their purpose is to make the audience's pupils contract slightly, to prevent them seeing the puppeteers.

The colourful appeal of ultra-violet lighting and fluorescent colours is very seductive. It is splendid for bright spectacle and special effects but some people find it tiring on the eyes to watch, or perform by, for long periods, and the colour is rarely subtle. Therefore, the alternative form, which uses white light, tends to be used for serious drama and UV is used most often for variety or pantomime-style pieces, although there are of course notable exceptions.

SOUND

Developments in the quality and compactness of sound systems, coupled with moderate prices, have revolutionized puppet theatre sound. A complete system can still be an expensive outlay, but reasonable equipment is essential.

Principles

Sound equipment may seem remarkably loud under home conditions, but in a large hall it may be barely audible, so amplification might be necessary.

With many systems it is recommended that separate loudspeakers are used, as built-in speakers often cannot cope with high volume without distortion. Larger extension speakers permit greater volume with better tone and less distortion, although there are some small loudspeakers with high-volume capabilities. Ensure the loudspeakers you select give good-quality speech reproduction as well as music.

Loudspeakers should be carefully positioned on each side of the stage in front of the curtains or the sound will be muffled. Some performers add a third speaker either just above or below the stage. It is important to check the acoustics in the auditorium and adjust the sound accordingly at each venue when setting up.

Sometimes loudspeakers in front of thick curtains cannot be heard easily by the performers back-stage. It is tempting to turn up the sound, but the front rows of the audience will suffer. Instead, have an extra loudspeaker back-stage for the puppeteers.

Any of the portable sound systems detailed below may be suitable, depending on your requirements, but take care to purchase equipment that is compatible, especially when using microphones and amplifiers. Make sure the system permits the use of the CD player, or tape deck, and microphone together, and that their relative volumes can be balanced. If there is to be a number of microphones, a mixer unit will be needed to blend and balance the various sources. Ensure that, at the required volumes and at the planned distance between microphone and loudspeakers, you do not get feedback, which will produce a terrible howl. Make sure your lighting control system does not cause an audible hum in the sound system and, wherever possible, plug the sound system into a different electrical outlet from that used for the lighting system.

Microphones

Choose a microphone carefully, as a poor one can ruin a performance. It might be a clip-on (lapel/tie) model, or a neck microphone, with a suitable halter so that it does not move while you are performing. It must pick up your speech clearly without your having to direct your mouth down towards it, and it must be capable of being used with a reasonable length of lead to the amplifier. If the lead is too short, you will be restricted but, with some microphones, increasing the length of the lead can result in interference.

A radio microphone liberates you from the restriction of a lead. It may be a clip-on or neck model, or worn like headphones; hand-held models are clearly not suitable for puppeteers. It will have a lead to a small transmitter carried on the belt or hip, and a remote receiver that plugs into an amplifier; some integrated systems are now available.

If you use a microphone, remember that *all* back-stage asides are amplified (and do not forget to switch off a radio microphone before using the loo!).

Sound Systems

The following sound systems cater for a range of budgets and performance needs.

CD OR CASSETTE TAPE PLAYER

Some larger units provide good sound reproduction, even without extension speakers. The volume may well be sufficient for small shows that do not need microphones. Of course, with a CD player you need recordable compact disks and access to a CD recorder.

CD OR CASSETTE TAPE DECK WITH AMPLIFIER AND LOUDSPEAKERS

A good-quality CD player or tape deck is important, used in conjunction with a compatible amplifier and loudspeakers. Hi-fi amplifiers are not sufficiently sturdy for the rigours of a travelling show, and may not be powerful enough anyway. A good public-address unit is preferable, but beware of cheaper models that give poor sound reproduction. The ability to mix music and live voice (via microphones) is highly desirable; some accept two microphones, but a mixing unit will be needed if additional microphones are used.

INTEGRATED SOUND SYSTEM

Certain manufacturers, particularly those catering for the education market, now produce complete units comprising cassette tape deck (and sometimes CD deck), microphone inputs, amplifier and loudspeaker, plus extension speaker sockets, all in one cabinet. They are compact, sturdy, reliable, powerful and excellent for transporting. To deter thieves, some are designed deliberately not to be attractive as a home sound system. Versions are available also with an integral radio-microphone system.

The development of karaoke entertainment has given rise to a range of similar units, with all manner of facilities, at quite reasonable prices. By comparison with those designed for the education market, cheaper karaoke units rarely match the sound quality, volume and sturdiness, they rarely have radio microphones, and they are more susceptible to theft, an important

Fig 196 (b) a Coomber radio microphone system incorporating (1) headband microphone or (2) lapel microphone, (3) bodypack transmitter and (4) radio microphone receiver unit;

Fig 196 (c) a high-power, Coomber public address/cassette recorder for larger areas. It has an integral radio-microphone system and an autofade facility that offers progressive reduction of the tape playback level when the microphone is used. Other versions are available with different power levels, with or without the radio-microphone system and other facilities

Fig 196 A selection of sound systems from the Coomber Electronic Equipment range – (a) this Coomber compact disc player/cassette recorder incorporates stereo loudspeakers and has inputs for microphones or a radio microphone system. It is sufficiently powerful for a school hall;

consideration for the travelling puppeteer. However, they might suit certain budgets and requirements.

Some specialist suppliers of audio equipment will customize a sound system within a sturdy trunk suitable for transport.

REEL-TO-REEL TAPE DECK WITH AMPLIFIER AND LOUDSPEAKERS

Reel-to-reel tape decks are preferred by some companies, in pursuit of high-quality sound. These are obviously larger and more cumbersome than cassette players, but some consider them to be worth the trouble and investment.

Their use would be pointless without high-quality amplification equipment. Those with speeds of 7.5 and 15 i.p.s. are preferable; the latter is better for quality in music reproduction and for editing purposes. However, the development of recordable compact disks, and their quality, is making large reel-to-reel decks redundant for performing.

9 The Performance

ESSENTIAL CONSIDERATIONS

If you plan to produce a puppet performance, you need to consider a number of very basic issues. First, why are you undertaking a puppet production? For whom is it intended? The answer to these questions will influence what you tackle, and a clear sense of your audience will also help you to select and to structure the performance appropriately.

Where are you to perform? Different types of venue have different facilities, space, blackout, and implications for the size of puppets and staging. Consider also the space available for construction, rehearsal and storage.

The time-scale for a production helps to determine how ambitious you can afford to be, and provides useful deadlines. Putting on a production will *always* take longer than you think, especially the construction, so the risk is that your performance will be under-rehearsed. Move the construction along fairly speedily to allow scope for developing the performance; the larger the group, the more time is generally needed to prepare the performance.

Apart from the 'gestation period', during which a project may simmer away for some months – even years –

Fig 197 *The Quest for Olwen*, designed and directed by John Blundall

before the work really begins, most companies allow at least a year to eighteen months to build a show; some take as long as four years. Time is needed to find the required materials, to construct each puppet, the staging and the scenery, to work on the text, and on the lighting and sound. Professionals also need to find time for the publicity and administration relating to a future show, as well as for performing their current show.

What will it cost? Or, what can you afford? Budget for materials, staging, lighting and sound equipment. Professionals must also consider transport, administration and publicity costs. People's time can be a major cost. If you commission a puppet that takes two weeks to make, then the cost of that single puppet is the cost of the materials, plus two weeks' work.

What talent is available and what talent is needed? Who is going to direct the production, write the script, tend to design and construction, prepare the music, manipulate and speak for the puppets? There are many one- and two-person companies who do it all themselves, but some use other sources too. For example, for their voice actors and musicians, they make use of the local community, school and youth orchestras, amateur dramatic groups, and so on.

What materials and equipment do you have and what more are needed? What transport is available? This influences your choice of staging, size of puppets, and how many people can be included in a travelling show. If the height of the puppets is increased by half, so are the dimensions of the props – $50 \times 50 \times 50$cm (0.125 cu.m.) becomes $75 \times 75 \times 75$cm (0.422 cu.m.) – and this increases the volume of what you must store and transport by nearly three and a half times.

How can you publicize the show effectively? Publicity can be both time-consuming and expensive. Some professional performers budget as much for promotion as for production costs – plus a lot of time. Even when you have an established reputation, you are only as good as your last show, and the best form of advertising is word of mouth. You need to maintain standards and spend a lot of time making and maintaining contacts. You must get in touch with the right people for the sort of show you are promoting, so research this thoroughly. Some national puppetry organizations produce directories, and it is worth being included in these. Local radio and television features help too, but remember that no *one* thing works; a combination of promotional measures is needed.

An attractive and informative brochure for potential venues is essential. Have the show's designer come up with the brochure, posters, programme, and so on, in order to achieve a unified image. The brochure should describe the show and reflect its style as accurately as possible; make clear your technical requirements, the price and any other details (such as travel expenses and accommodation, if applicable). It is good practice always to have written agreements and to take an invoice to the venue in case it is required. Do all you can to facilitate the payment of your fees, but be prepared for delays in payment.

If a show is successful, clearly this is a prime target for future publicity, but remember that, if you are re-engaged by the same venue, you will need a new show and, if you return too often, you will ruin your scarcity value.

Finally, if you are engaging in public performances, you must check copyright and performing rights payments due, and you must ensure that you comply with fire regulations and other health and safety or licensing requirements. (Fireproofing materials are available from theatrical suppliers.) You will also need insurance for the puppets, staging and props, lighting and sound equipment, transport, the puppeteers and the audience (public liability). Never take chances.

VARIETY SHOWS

Traditionally, shows consisting of variety or circus acts have used marionettes, but all types of puppet can

Fig 198 Albrecht Roser's *Clown Gustaf*

perform variety turns. It is especially popular among solo puppeteers, for whom plays may be more problematic to mount.

The staging may be simple or elaborate, and acts can be adapted for both adults and children. A programme might comprise a sketch or two and various acts involving tricks and transformations. Sketches need not be elaborate; it is the idea and its execution that matter. Precision timing and skilful manipulation can make it highly effective.

Popular turns include clowns, strong man, juggler, extending or collapsible puppet, acrobat, monocyclist, reversible puppet, dual-controlled dancers, contortionist, trapeze artist, stilt walker, lion and lion tamer, puppet puppeteer, and come-apart puppets (for example, a dissecting skeleton). Performing animals are popular with audiences and can be used to perform most of these acts. You can also design a puppet to perform different acts – a tight-rope walker can be a contortionist, and a juggler can be an extending puppet.

Each turn has to be fitted into an act; this requires ingenuity and imagination, in addition to working out the technicalities of puppet construction and control. The dissecting skeleton cannot just walk on, come apart and walk off. If the puppet is to ride a monocycle, what will it do while on it? Avoid copying other performers and create your own act.

Puppets may simply perform to music or may talk directly to the audience or to other puppets. All these techniques may be employed within the same show, depending on the acts. If a show needs to be of a certain length, involving audience participation, you might need a few 'filler' acts, which may be used depending on time.

Much of the advice below is relevant to both plays and variety, but timing and precision in all elements are of supreme importance. Variety should not be rushed, but it must also never be allowed to drag.

PLAYS

There is a common consensus that puppets should do that which they do well, and not attempt that which the live actor can do better. There must be a reason for presenting the piece with puppets; the puppets must bring something to the piece, so short stories tend to work better than long. With the latter, all you can do is cut it down.

Puppets also need to work in the here-and-now, and in concrete terms. They cannot philosophize, and cannot reflect on the past; they must be in the moment or moving forward. This is a fundamental principle: the audience must do the philosophizing, not the puppet.

It is worth noting how much of puppet theatre originates with the narrative form. Good live plays are often not good puppet plays, and playwrights seldom write well for puppets. Good stories do not always make good plays either; you must consider the dramatic content. What sort of imagery does it contain? How much of the story can be translated directly into action? Puppets that stand still and talk are not interesting to watch.

Writing an original play involves the development of a plot, settings and characters, from which a scenario and script can be created. The most difficult aspect of this is undoubtedly the plot itself, and there is no simple formula; plays for puppets are not universally reducible to certain elements, but a number of principles may be suggested.

Principles for Adapting a Story

First, construct a brief outline of the story and determine the physical shape of the production – the kind of puppets you are going to use, and so on. You may wish to retain the style and essence of the source, and as much original dialogue as appropriate. Some stories demand a good deal of inventiveness from the writer, whereas the dialogue of others just seems to flow. Never lose sight of the need for action, however.

The process of adaptation requires certain preliminary steps. First, are there any events that do little to move the plot forward or develop the characters? These might be deleted. Are any characters superfluous? Are any events or situations difficult to depict with puppets? Can these be deleted or, if essential, how could they be achieved or suggested? It may be necessary to do away with, or combine, some of the characters and places of action, confining the piece to three or four scenes. Additionally, are there in the text any brief but important scenes that need elaboration? This particular task needs a good deal of care.

At what point in the story should the play open? It need not start where the book does; what will have the best dramatic impact, without confusing or boring the audience? A good deal has to be achieved in this opening scene, in terms of story and character development, atmosphere, and so on.

Cutting down does not mean reducing everything to a single simple storyline; this would trivialize the piece. There must be development of character and plot; there may also be a subplot. In a sense, writing for puppet theatre is rather like writing a good book for children – a children's book needs to achieve all that has to be achieved in an adult book, but with far fewer words. Similarly, puppet theatre is drama condensed.

The Scenario and Script

Having chosen your material and prepared an outline of the story, develop the scenario – an account of who does what, and where. It is useful to include preliminary stage directions too. Some performers start with a storyboard – a series of pictures depicting the main steps in the development of the story – and then fill in the gaps.

From the outset, keep in mind the shape of the play. Note each development vital to the plot, and arrange the whole series of actions in the most telling order. Ensure that all important action takes place on-stage; it is not appropriate for a character to enter and say what he has just done off-stage if this is an essential aspect of the plot. Although Shakespeare uses explanatory dialogue in his prologues, in order to set the scene, it seldom works with puppets. The audience needs to *see* the important action. A play that opens with two puppets giving a lengthy exposition is both clumsy and boring;

such a scene does not make good puppet theatre.

Decide which characters are essential to the development of the plot. Keep the stage clear of those that are not important, and keep to a minimum the number of manipulators required in any scene. Manipulators need much more space than puppets, so beware of crowd scenes.

Decide where the climax comes and make sure that no intermediate action detracts from it; remember that, if the audience is to participate fully in the climax, they must understand how it came about. To have recourse to explanations at the end is highly undesirable.

Variety of pace and emotion are essential. The audience cannot sustain a high level of emotion throughout, and it does not make good theatre. Hitchcock created suspense not by surprise after surprise, but by building, changing pace, and juxtaposing. Comedy may be pointed up by a subdued moment, and tragedy can be heightened by light relief. Treat the writing with great care, however; do not let it become ludicrous, and destroy the continuity of the play. The audience must be kept interested in what is coming next.

It is very good practice for the first character to enter and *do* something as soon as the curtain goes up. It is not usually a good idea to start explaining the plot the moment the play starts. For the first minute or two many people do not really listen to puppets; they are too busy watching – taking in the type of puppet, method of operation, and the conventions of the performance.

Different types of puppet, and the size and shape of the staging, will offer possibilities, but will also impose restrictions. These two factors might determine whether, for example, you

Fig 199 *Peer Gynt*, a shadow production by the Little Angel Theatre

can write in action that requires great height or width.

Do not plan scenes that require long scene-changes; the audience may become restless, and it will be difficult to sustain the mood or the flow of the production. Have as few breaks as possible (most performances do not have an interval), and either change settings in full view, choreographed as part of the performance, or try to limit scene-changes to two minutes; under no circumstances should they be longer than three minutes.

The step from the scenario to the final script can be taken in a variety of ways. If the piece originated with a script, clearly the scenario and final text will have developed together. In identifying the major elements of the scenario, you will also have been identifying the significant aspects of the script. Now you need the links to enable the play to flow with continuity.

If the play originated with a text, storyline or other theme, you can proceed in one of two ways: either have a suitably experienced writer convert the scenario into a script; or use a process of improvisation, which is recorded, transcribed and then adapted and refined as necessary. Puppets should be used for any improvisation, even if the actual figures are not yet made. It is not wise to use human acting as a basis for puppet acting, as speech tends to dominate action.

While working on the text – editing, juxtaposing, writing text where necessary to make the links – try to see the piece visually in your head. Think about it in terms of stage action, music, projections, and so on. Construct a mental picture of the total piece, not just the words.

Try to find the appropriate level for the dialogue. Challenge the audience and do not patronize them. Most peo-

Fig 200 The Devil from Stravinsky's *A Soldier's Tale*, the Little Angel Theatre

ple have experienced puppet shows where shrill voices recite sloppy dialogue. Too much puppet dialogue is there to fill in time, with no shape or direction or good purpose to it. Whoever writes your script must have a sound knowledge of what puppets do well and what they do badly, and a grasp of puppetry fundamentals – such as the need to avoid long speeches. They need to have seen a range of puppet theatre and worked with puppets themselves. There is no substitute for first-hand experience, and the writer will find it immensely helpful to have been involved in directing a puppet production.

Writers not experienced with puppets may find it difficult to compress action into a few sentences. One mistake is to go through a lot of dialogue –

or wrapping – in order to get to the point. The secret is to make the audience work, and not to do it all for them. You present the word, the music, the image – you set it up, but you let them discover what is going on inside the puppet's head or its heart, what the ideas are in the sub-text, and so on.

There are many ways to involve your audience. Most important is how you hint or suggest, inviting the audience to supply with the imagination those other dimensions that puppets cannot achieve. The way in which the audience brings something to the performance is a powerful aspect of puppet theatre; some shows do not succeed, because they demand nothing from the audience. Audience involvement is not just about verbal participation (which can make children become quite uncontrolled); the puppeteer should be able to play on the audience, to invite them to think and to feel, to move them in the ways in which they are moved by live actors.

Consider how to conclude the play. Sometimes this is not at all clear. The curtain drops and the house lights come up, but nothing inherent in the performance signals effectively that the play has finished. You do not need some naive line that says, 'well, that's the end', but the style of ending, the use of music and lighting, together with the way in which the story concludes – and the posed stage picture – should be able to communicate effectively that the piece has ended. Once the drama has been resolved, do not draw out the finale, or the impact will be lost. Bring down the curtain fairly soon.

Finally, be disciplined about the length of your show. Many puppet shows would be much improved by dramatic tightening up, and a reduction in length.

Design and Construction

A good deal of thought and discussion needs to go into the design of your show, especially if you have outside help. The brief may be for puppets, sets and staging, or for only certain aspects. You may be using an existing stage, and seeking help with the design of puppets and scenery; you may be confident in these areas, but need help with the actual dimensions and shape of the performing area, in order to set up the space in the most effective way.

Some performers start the design and the making of the puppets after the text or the scenario is written and the mode of staging is decided. For others, the puppets come first. Whichever way you proceed, you need to have an overall design concept and to determine the puppets' sizes and relative sizes. Then you can finalize designs, and start construction.

Design involves a range of considerations: can the number of performers manage all that is required? What can be afforded? What technical aspects relate to what the puppets are required to do? Different considerations have implications for design and possibly also for the storyline or script.

While construction proceeds, some performers use existing puppets or lay figures to work on the performance, but the actual ones are preferable. Even if they are not finished, if they are in a workable state, you can start to rehearse. A run-through at this stage may reveal problems and save a lot of adjustments later.

Lighting must be designed too: it may be simple but you still have to decide where to put the lights, colour for different effects and how proposed costumes and scenery will appear under stage lighting.

Music for the Show

Music is used to enhance mood and atmosphere, to link scenes and bridge intervals, so that these qualities are sustained, but it should not force itself upon an audience. There are good dramatic reasons for having no music at times, but there are equally good reasons for including it elsewhere. The question is: what does it do for this particular piece?

Choose the music before rehearsals, then time it in rehearsal and adjust it as the performance takes shape. The final performance recording should be ready by the last week of rehearsal. Ensure that the reproduction quality is good. Live music is usually too difficult to arrange but, when it is possible, it brings a whole new dimension to a production.

You may precede curtain-up with a short appropriate piece, but music at the end of a performance may detract from the effect of the final curtain. Sometimes, however, a variety finale can be given a final polish by a suitable piece played after the curtain falls.

It pays always to listen to music with a critical ear, noting down what certain passages suggest to you and how certain pieces might be used. Compact discs are particularly helpful, as they enable you to check and note precisely where the passage can be found. Keeping a reference book full of notes can save considerable time when music is needed.

Fig 201 Two types of rod puppet used in open-stage style for Barry Smith's Theatre of Puppets production of *Starchild*

Voice Work and Recording Techniques

LIVE VOICE OR RECORDED DIALOGUE

You do not need to put on funny voices for puppets. You need to breathe properly and to project the voice well and clearly. You must be very crisp and clean in your speech tunes and rhythms. You must have very clear changes of intervals in the voice (in the musical sense) to match the changes of thought. There is much to be gained by taking lessons from a good voice teacher.

You do need a character voice, however; one excellent example is the voice work in Disney films, which demonstrates the sort of technique you need. First, read the text aloud in your normal voice, then experiment with different character voices to find one that is both appropriate for the puppet and comfortable for you.

Do not use recorded dialogue unless it is really necessary, and you have high-quality recording facilities. A poor recording will ruin the show, and technical hitches while the dialogue runs on can reduce a serious piece to farce. Live voice has a better capacity to hold the attention of the audience and can also allow for audience response and participation. However, plays which require a puppeteer to create a variety of character voices while operating puppets within a curtained stage – and possibly a number of times a day – present physical problems, even with the use of a microphone. High-quality recorded dialogue can therefore make possible an otherwise impossible task. Remember, though, if something goes wrong on stage, you have little scope for improvisation. Also, once you are performing a show, it is much more problematic to make any changes when dialogue is recorded.

RECORDING TECHNIQUES

If you *are* recording dialogue, ideally you should use a recording studio (which can be very expensive) and create tracks for voice, music and background effects – both general effects that create atmosphere, and spot effects, such as a door opening or a clock chiming. Of course, this is beyond the resources of most performers; alternatively, use the best-quality compact disk or recording tape available, and record tapes on standard play, not long play. Test the acoustics wherever you are to record; a comfortably furnished, carpeted room with plenty of drapes and other fabrics will give better reproduction than an empty hall with bare walls and hard floors. Whatever your circumstances, select from the following stages as appropriate to your needs and aim for the best quality within your resources.

RECORDING THE VOICE TRACK

Let the voice actors handle, and improvise with, the puppets; this will make a difference to their performance. Ensure that they have rehearsed the play thoroughly before the recording and be warned that the whole process is *very* time consuming: you will be lucky if four hours of recording produces thirty minutes of performance dialogue and it could take two or three weeks to edit a thirty minute professional quality voice track. Limit the recording sessions to about four hours per day: longer produces diminishing returns.

Break down the text into sections of an appropriate size for recording, and open each 'take' with a spoken identifier (for example, Section 1, Take 3). Keep all the takes. You can select from them and edit them to achieve the best voice track possible; also, you might need to re-mix the master when the show has been performed.

MIXING THE MASTER RECORDING

When you come to mix the master version, heed the advice of Ray DaSilva: 'It is like painting a picture: if you put on too many layers, it gets muddy. When I am preparing the background, I might decide to have a clock ticking away all the time, which the audience will be aware of as the scene starts, but then I take it right down so you can hardly hear it, but it is just there. There might be gaps in the scene where there is suspense or where somebody is walking about or thinking, where I might bring up that little bit of background. I record sufficient of that background to keep it running all the time I am doing the mixing so that I can just bring it up and down when I want to.

'Clearly, re-editing a master recording can have a series of implications, so

Fig 202 *Peter and the Wolf* by the DaSilva Puppet Company uses many types of puppet. Here Peter is a 'body puppet' and the wolf is a rod-marionette. Peter's head, hands and boots are cast in latex rubber; the body, upper arms and legs (with webbing joints) have plywood centres with foam rubber padding on the back and front. Thick control rods through the elbows form the forearms and are secured in the hands. Shaped plywood strips attach the puppet's soles to the puppeteer's shoes. A plastic ball is inserted into the head for strength and to maintain its shape. Head strings are attached to the puppeteer's head-ring, and shoulder strings attach to a strap looped round her neck. The wolf has a modelled head, with a hinged jaw and a sculpted polystyrene body built upon a plywood profile shape. The plywood is hinged vertically with door hinges to provide the required flexibility

have reference points within it: this might be a silent pause, a note of music or a point where there is only one track being fed on at that moment, so if you want to alter three or four words, you might have to alter only a relatively short part of the master recording.'

Although it is not easy to achieve, audience response *can* be anticipated and accommodated, not by leaving gaps but by having something there that does not matter if, for example, it is covered by audience laughter. Music

may be used, or even dialogue, if it is not essential. If no reaction occurs, the puppet continues to move appropriately to the background music; it may look thoughtful, or it may simply continue to perform with the covering dialogue.

Manipulation and Movement

Good manipulation requires total concentration by the puppeteer, so keep your eyes on your puppet and act *through* it. When you have the same focus as the puppet, a better quality of movement is achieved. You will need, therefore, to know the play thoroughly, as you cannot use a script when performing. Also watch the eye-line of the puppets so that they are inter-relating realistically; think about where the puppet is focusing. Pace and timing are also important, so think quickly, but take your time.

One thing at a time is another rule. Do not wiggle the puppets about, or slur all the movements together. As John Wright advised, 'Every line should have an action and every action should have a meaning. Never put in unnecessary movement.' Puppet theatre is more akin to mime and dance than to human theatre, and a puppet's movements should be crisp, clean-cut and drawn in the air very precisely, like those of a dancer. Generally, the principle is *new moves on new thoughts.*

To make each puppet exciting to watch and convincing in its role, it is important to try to introduce as much variation of gesture as possible, within the limits of characterization. When exploring the range of movement and gesture, you might perform the play yourself entirely in mime. The limitations of speechlessness force you to explore a wider range of action and gesture; then your task is to try to achieve those movements with the puppet. Also, study gestures and try to relate them to emotions. Remember that it is the *whole* puppet that communicates character and emotion, not just the head and hands.

Economy of movement and economy of gesture are essential. It helps to have plenty of intrinsic movement in the puppet and its costume, so that you supply just what is required, and let the puppet's natural movements do as much as possible for you.

Consider how to indicate which puppet is speaking. If the audience is

Fig 203 *Sleeping Beauty* with puppets carved by John Wright, the Little Angel Theatre

to believe that the puppet is speaking, words and actions must synchronize and it must be possible to tell which puppet is speaking other than by recognizing its voice. Subdue the actions of the figures that are silent (without allowing them to appear lifeless), so that all attention is focused on the speaking character. The silent figures can make appropriately subdued gestures, such as nods of assent, directed towards the speaker.

The convention of moving the speaking puppet is often carried too far, with it nodding or jiggling to every syllable of speech. Use the puppet's movements to emphasize just the important words or phrases, as people do. If the puppet has a moving mouth, note the advice on hand puppets in Chapter 5. Lip synchronization is a difficult skill to master while also concentrating on the overall puppet movement. A fine example of expert technique is the Muppet Show.

Ensure that glove and rod puppets do not disappear from view as they move about the acting area. As the playboard is usually higher than the audience, the puppets will appear to sag below the stage level as they move up-stage (away from the audience), unless they are raised slightly to compensate. Also, establish the height above the playboard of glove and rod puppets, and in relation to each other, and keep them walking on the same level. This problem is compounded by the varying heights of the operators. Try not to operate sitting down, as this is very limiting.

Pay attention to the way the puppet takes and leaves the stage. Do not swing a marionette on to the stage, or make rod and glove puppets pop up out of the floor. For a good entrance, the puppet should be in action before it appears. Use doorways, arches and wings to bring the puppet to the appropriate height *out of sight*, and then walk it into view. In a booth with none of these devices, it is a good idea to imagine a set of stairs and have the puppet walk up these into view. The same applies to exits.

You can use a mirror for practice, but this has its limitations. It will help you check details, but the most important skill to acquire is how to *feel* when the puppet is not moving appropriately. Over-dependence on a mirror hinders the acquisition of this skill and prevents proper concentration on the puppet. Take advice from a director, let the performers take turns sitting in the auditorium and, where possible, make good use of a video-recorder. However, do not do this too early in rehearsals, as it can be demoralizing.

Pay sufficient attention to the movement of those puppets whose characters are more difficult to portray (witches and villains are often much easier than princesses and heroes). Make full use of the conventions of puppet theatre, where puppets do not have to do everything themselves; puppeteers in view of the audience can always act on behalf of the puppet.

Very difficult actions can draw undue attention to themselves, either by being bungled *or* by being performed with ease (to the amazement of the audience). By drawing attention to the puppet as a puppet, these can break the atmosphere of a play. Variety acts may thrive on provoking the audience's admiration, but the audience at a play should not be distracted by a clever piece of production.

When manipulating to recorded dialogue, the puppeteers should not be struggling to keep up with the tape. They need to know the tape so thoroughly that they are ahead of it; they have to know what their next line is going to be so that they can set it up.

The puppet's movement should anticipate the word, not follow it. Although appearing almost simultaneous, there is actually a finely constructed sequence to convincing movement and speech. The puppet thinks, then moves, then delivers the line. It does not deliver the line before the accompanying movement.

The manipulation and movement of individual puppets must be viewed and choreographed in relation to the overall stage picture and to the movements of other characters. This is part of the business of rehearsal.

Rehearsal

Rehearsal involves taking a broad view of the play, getting the underlying structure right, then looking at smaller and smaller units to refine the detail, and finally putting the whole together again. Considerable time may be spent cutting down to the minimum necessary to achieve the desired effect. Some puppeteers do too much – too much acting, too much talking, and for too long.

Adequate rehearsal is essential for perfecting technique, developing confidence, resolving technical and production problems, and considering aspects of design, lighting, sound, scenery and costume. Rehearsal should never be rushed; two hours is usually as much as the performers can take without a break, and about six hours a day in total. Allow at least thirty to thirty-five hours' rehearsal for every fifteen minutes of playing time.

If one person has conceived, designed, constructed and prepared the piece, it might benefit from a fresh, objective view, which may pick up on shortcomings that have been 'lived with' as the performance has taken

shape. Think about inviting someone from outside to direct, or at least to offer constructive criticism.

The manipulators must be thoroughly familiar with a play before rehearsals begin. They should have taken part in read-throughs of the script and discussed the text and the characters.

The first priority in rehearsal is 'blocking' – constructing a general scheme for movement about the stage so that people know where the puppets are going. Also, start to make notes of stage management requirements. At this stage the director is not concerned with the gestures of the individual characters, but with the overall patterns of movement; the aim is to arrange groups and position individual puppets to the best visual and dramatic effect. Relative position, as well as individual movement and gesture, conveys a good deal about mood, attitudes and what is happening between the characters.

Fig 204 shows the six major stage positions: down-centre is the strongest, followed by up-centre, then down-right and down-left. Up-right and up-left are the weakest positions, and not usually suitable for major action. The major character will often utilize the

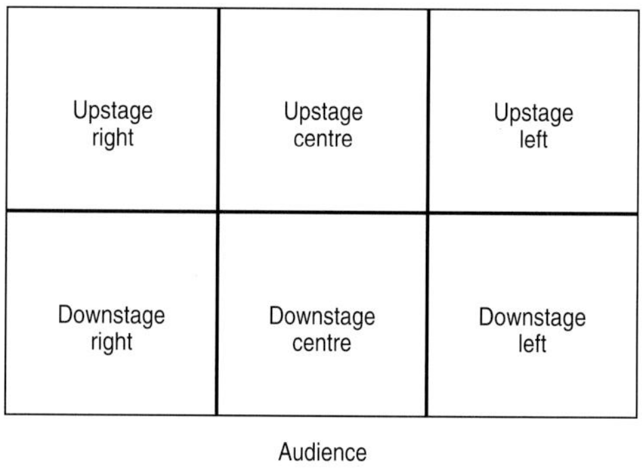

Upstage right	Upstage centre	Upstage left
Downstage right	Downstage centre	Downstage left

Audience

Fig 204 The main stage positions

area down-centre, or down-right or down-left, but you should aim for variety in the use of space.

Until people have the confidence of knowing where they are, and are familiar with their entrances and exits, and bigger issues concerned with props and stage management, they cannot focus on the acting of their puppet. If issues of detail regarding individual performances arise, make a note of them and come back to them later.

Every move or series of moves is noted in the master script and simple diagrams illustrating these are drawn opposite the appropriate speeches. Having established the major positions, you can work within that framework.

Decide on the basic actions of the individual characters; introduce their most important gestures and determine the cues for them. To this foundation add details of action and build the complete pattern of the puppet's movement, so that it flows smoothly from one position to the next. In puppet theatre you have to work hard at continuity; every movement has to be a preparation for the next, so work on achieving the effects you want *and* getting them flowing, but always with regard for the overall stage picture.

Puppets do not need always to walk directly from one spot to another. Their paths might sometimes involve a circular pattern or a loop; make the most of the space and let the puppets use it to the full. However, be careful not to have characters crossing one another all the time; having to manoeuvre past each other at every cross-over will cause problems for the manipulators.

The puppeteers' own movements should be worked out at this point and off-stage positions fixed for the puppets so that they can be found without

Fig 205 The Fisherman and the Devil from the Little Angel Theatre's production of Oscar Wilde's *The Fisherman and his Soul*. The Devil was designed by Lyndie Wright, the Fisherman by John Wright, who carved both figures in wood

hesitation. The back-stage choreography is of immense importance.

The puppets need to relate to one another but do not let them 'upstage' each other – do not position a figure so that another has to turn its back to the audience to deliver a line - and do not let them permanently present a profile to the audience. Position them so that they can relate to each other by turning about 45 degrees. As you develop the movement, watch your lighting areas and make sure that one puppet does not steal another's light.

Blocking can take up one-third of rehearsal time, then another third might be spent focusing upon smaller units; the remaining third would be devoted to building it up again and getting it right. By now you should have built up a 'muscular memory', so that your fingers are always ahead. The last three or four days' rehearsal should be devoted to running the complete show, stopping where necessary to look at detail, but in relation to the total package. It is important that a play is rehearsed sufficiently *as a whole*.

Rehearsal involves also the delegation of stage-management tasks to be covered during the performance. Usually, everybody does everything, although major characters might be operated by particular members of the company, and a very complicated lighting scheme with frequent changes might demand its own operator. The organization of these tasks is all part of the back-stage choreography. Each performer will have his or her own individual schedule of tasks, for example:

Scene 3:   Standby on bridge.

Take puppet from DC. Hang on rack and check.

Work owl in tree after clouds disappear.

2, 5, 6 down to 25 per cent (lighting change) when wolf appears.

Interval: Remove tree and fence.

Place rocks in circle, centre stage.

At the technical rehearsal, do not run through the whole dialogue, but practise curtain cues, lighting cues, music cues and sound cues. Check very basic details, such as the space for entrances and exits. Setting out the puppets, props and scenery should all be practised until they are instinctive, as should the setting up and 'striking' (taking down) of the stage, so that the whole operation becomes smooth and efficient.

Scene-changes should be timed and rehearsed until they are as smooth as the rest of the performance, and no unintended sounds should be heard by the audience. Soft-soled shoes are essential. Another routine matter is the checking of all equipment, examining all puppets, controls, strings, scenery and props before and after each rehearsal or show. Checking the packing or unpacking of puppets, properties and other equipment is facilitated if a list is kept.

An emergency kit containing a small selection of tools, fuses, glue, tape, and so on, should always be kept handy (and tidy), in case running repairs are necessary.

The Performance

All elements of construction and preparation are united in the performance; it is the moment when all aspects of the puppeteer's art are on show, and it is essential that this work should be shown to its best advantage. From the moment the performers arrive for an engagement they are on show, and they must be professional throughout.

You might send a reminder card to the venue, to confirm the details of arrival and performance times, and any facilities agreed. Ensure your equipment is in first-class order *and* appearance, and that your transport is in good running order. It is *essential* to arrive on time, to set up efficiently and to be ready to perform on time.

No venue will be ideal, but do not complain about its shortcomings; make the best of the situation you find. Be prepared for every type of electrical socket and carry metres and metres of cable; sockets always seem to be in the worst possible places. Be totally self-

sufficient and aim never to ask to borrow anything.

During the show there must be *complete* silence back-stage. Even whispers can carry, and will spoil the illusion being created.

It is debatable among puppeteers whether performers should allow themselves to be seen after the show — assuming they have not been working in the open. Some come forward to take a bow, some come forward with one of the puppets, others prefer to remain unseen. The question is whether the magic and illusion of the puppets would be destroyed by the appearance of its performers. The decision is yours.

After the first few performances of a new production, pause to take a fresh look at the whole show, to reassess it in the light of how the audiences have received it. If there are any improvements that can be made, do make them, and do not be satisfied with anything less than perfection. Every effort should be made to improve the standard of any production. The show reflects and represents months, perhaps years, of work, but it is by the finished production that the puppeteer's work is judged.

Finally, enjoy your puppetry and every success with your puppet theatre productions!

Fig 206 Marionettes from *Alice in Wonderland* by the DaSilva Puppet Company. The figures are approximately 1.2m (4ft) high. Alice has a cast latex-rubber head with an internal 'dowelling cross' (*see* page 47) and a plywood and foam rubber body. The Gryffin's head and Mock Turtle's head and body are modelled, while the Gryffin's body is fabric over wood and foam rubber. Legs and feet are a mixture of padded plywood, carved wood and modelling

Useful Addresses

There are national and regional puppet theatre organizations throughout the world as well as the international puppet theatre organisation, UNIMA (*L'Union Internationale de la Marionnette*) which has centres or sections in many countries. If you have any difficulty in finding what organizations, collections, puppet theatres, performances or courses ·exist in your area, a telephone call or a stamped, self-addressed envelope/international reply coupon to one of the following will help you to make local contact:

The Puppet Centre Trust
BAC
Lavender Hill
London
SW11 5TN
Tel: 0171 228 5335
Director: Loretta Howells
Open to visitors 2–6pm weekdays; telephone and postal information and advice service 10am–6pm weekdays.

Museum, collections, exhibitions; reference library including books, videos, slides, photographs, posters; publications, including *Animations* magazine; performances and events; educational projects and residencies; demonstrations and workshops; mail order catalogue for publications and puppetry-related merchandise

The Scottish Mask and Puppet Theatre Centre
8–10 Balcarres Avenue
Kelvindale
Glasgow
G12 0QF
Tel: 0141 339 6185
Fax: 0141 357 4484
Executive Director: Malcolm Knight
Public information, advice and sales 10am–5pm Mon–Sat, or by appointment.

Reference library including books, audio-visual material, poster and print collection; publications; performance programmes; education, therapy and special needs programmes; exhibitions; training, workshops and master classes; film and special effects workshop

British Puppet and Model Theatre Guild
Membership Secretary: Judith Shutt
Little Holme
Church Lane
Thames Ditton
Surrey
KT7 0NL

Membership organization with meetings in London and the provinces; weekend schools and panel of consultants; library and publications.

UNIMA British Centre
Membership Secretary: Martin MacGilp
10 Cullernie Gardens
Balloch
Inverness
IV2 7JP

International, non-governmental, membership organization with consultative status at UNESCO; 'brings together people from around the world who contribute to the art of puppetry'; publications; consultant service; events, international exchanges, collaborative projects; international festival and Congress every four years.

Further Reading
As bibliographies date very quickly, you are advised to consult one of the above organizations or the bookseller below for specialist advice and details of the latest books. This will also help you to find important texts that may no longer be generally available.

Ray DaSilva,
Supplier of Puppet Books
63 Kennedy Road
Bicester
Oxfordshire
OX6 8BE
Tel/Fax: 01869 245793

A specialist bookseller with a mail order catalogue that includes new and second-hand books.

Index